What Christian Leaders Are Saying . . .

"Sheri is an incredible person with an incredible story to tell."
Tony Cox, *Inside Edition*

"Sheri's life story is inspirational. She is a wonderful example of how God can completely change a person's heart and life."
Christine Core, Editor, *Role Model Magazine*

"Sheri Rose Shepherd is a stellar example of God's sovereign hand changing a life from hopelessness and despair to shining purpose and grace."
Jackie Mitchum Yockey, *The 700 Club*

"Sheri had the most incredible impact on our women and we now have the awesome privilege of following up with them. Thank you!"
Rene Dearie, Skyline Wesleyan Church,
Lemon Grove, California

"Sheri's anointed message draws people to receive the Crown of Life."
Kathy Arrington, Concerned Women for America

"Sheri's fresh anointing and great sense of humor brings individuals away from themselves and their difficulties to come to face to face with the Lord Jesus Christ."
Reverend Stanley Siwek, First Assembly of God,
White Plains, New York

"Sheri's warm and sincere personality inspires all who meet her. She is a true professional."
Tony Sepulveda, Lorimar Television

"Sheri is an inspiration to people of any age who have had to fight a battle in their life."
Talk TV Weekly

4263-55
0-8054-6355-0

Dewey Decimal Classification: B
Subject Heading: BEAUTY PAGEANT CONTEST—BIOGRAPHY
Library of Congress Card Catalog Number: 97-28083

Unless otherwise stated all Scripture citation is from the Revised
Standard Version of the Bible, copyrighted 1946, 1952, © 1971, 1973.
Other versions used are marked NASB, the New American Standard
Bible, © the Lockman Foundation, 1960, 1962, 1963, 1968, 1971,
1972, 1973, 1975, 1977,used by permission; and NIV, the Holy Bible,
New International Version, copyright © 1973, 1978, 1984 by
International Bible Society.

Library of Congress Cataloging-in-Publication Data
Shepherd, Sheri Rose, 1961–
    Life is not a dress rehearsal / Sheri Rose Shepherd ;
    with John Perry.
        p.   cm.
    ISBN 0-8054-6355-0 (pb)
    1. Shepherd, Sheri Rose, 1961– . 2. Beauty contestants—
United States—Biography. 3. Christian biography—United States.
I. Perry, John, 1952– . II. Title.
BR1725.S463A3   1997
277.3'0825'092
[B]—dc21

                                                    97-28083
                                                    CIP

1 2 3 4 5 01 00 99 98 97

Table of Contents

Contents

Acknowledgments

I'm so grateful to Broadman and Holman, especially editor Matt Jacobson, for giving me the opportunity to write this book. Thank you, John Perry, for taking my crazy life and putting it on paper in such a creative way. To my ministry staff, Tanna and Lana: I couldn't do what I do without your love, support, and incredible organizational skills.

Thank you, Dad, for believing in me when I didn't believe in myself. Thank you, Mom, for forgiving me and being a part of my life again. To Susie, my stepmom: God gave you the gift to love the unlovable. Because of your love and sacrifice, I'm who I am today.

And to my precious boys, my husband Steven and my son Jacob Andrew: I'm so grateful I get to share my life with you.

Introduction

My introduction to the world of public speaking and ministry, like so much of my life, was not exactly normal.

I was at a reunion dinner with my husband, Steve, sitting at a big table with about twenty of his friends from seminary. Generally speaking, I'm generally speaking, and on this occasion I was chatting pleasantly as usual with various people nearby. Suddenly, I heard a loud voice booming from across the table.

"Sheri Rose."

A little startled, I looked up at the stranger calling my name. Unable to ignore a voice reminiscent of a Boeing 747 beginning its takeoff run, the others looked up too.

"Sheri Rose, I heard you were a fat, Jewish, drug-addicted teenager from a broken home. How in the world did you ever become a Christian beauty queen? That's amazing!"

What's amazing, I thought to myself, *is how fast and at what volume this lady has just shared the Cliffs Notes version of my life with an entire restaurant. Wonder if she'd be willing to discuss some of the juicier details of her life?*

Around the table the crunching of croutons abruptly stopped, and all eyes turned to me. It wasn't exactly the kind of opening I was looking for to share my testimony, but it was the one God laid out before me at the moment, and I owed it to Him to answer . . . somehow. After a short pause, I said that I would share my story with them.

I told how I had been raised in a violent, dysfunctional home. I explained how God had rescued me from a miserable life as an overweight, insecure, severely bulimic young woman. I also recounted my darkest hour, when I was about to take my own life—how I cried out to God, and He answered. As I was sharing, I realized

2

how far God had brought me. We spent the rest of the evening laughing together, crying together, and sharing the joy of victory only Christ can bring to a life.

Driving home that night, I began to have second thoughts about what I'd said. The more I pondered, the more ashamed I became of all the mistakes I'd made. I wasn't proud of my poor choices; I wished I could re-live my life. That's when I began to realize that my life was not a dress rehearsal. I won't have a chance to do it over. How could God possibly be glorified by a past like mine?

A few weeks later, I picked up the phone to hear, "Hello, Sheri Rose." The roar of Miss 747 was unmistak-able. She said that she was with a national women's min-istry that was coming to Phoenix. Her speaker for the event had canceled, and she wanted to know if I would come and share my story with four hundred of her lead-ers who would be gathering from all over the nation.

"I can't," I said.

"Why not?"

"People like me don't speak in Christian circles. Besides, I'm not trained as a speaker. I don't even have a college degree."

"That doesn't matter."

"I'm too embarrassed. There is no way that I am going to come and share publicly all the mistakes that I ever made and how God had to fix them."

She had heard all the excuses she could take. "Sheri Rose," she thundered, "God did not pull you out of that dark place for you to keep it to yourself. He pulled you out so that you could pull others out too."

I thought, *This lady is either hearing from God or she's manipulating me.* Whichever it was, she got her way.

Before my speech I was so petrified I went to the bathroom seven times. I got so tired of walking back and forth between the head table and the ladies' room, I decided to stay put in the bathroom stall until it was time for me to speak. While waiting for the dinner to be over, I heard a woman behind a closed door say, "I am so stuffed, and now we have to sit and listen to that speaker!"

I was mortified. I came out of the stall and asked the ladies if they were with the same organization I was. They said, "No, we're with the pharmaceutical convention next door." *Whew!*

As I headed back down the hall to the meeting room, I heard the master of ceremonies introducing me. I ran up onto the podium and turned to face the four hundred pairs of eyes looking back at me. With my knees knocking together like castanets, I started retelling the story I had shared at Steve's reunion dinner. I said everything I could think of and still took only fifteen minutes of the forty-five they gave me, then ran off the stage and back to the bathroom. I thanked God I would never have to do that again.

Wrong!

A few weeks later my phone started ringing with requests to come speak at women's retreats, women's conferences, and church services. I couldn't believe it! Isn't it amazing how God can take our messy lives and turn them into a ministry for His glory? He will if we allow Him to!

Time after time, my experiences have reminded me that life is not a practice run. None of us have an opportunity to go through it all again. Each day, good or bad, we have the choice of giving our best performance for the glory of God. It's our choices, not chance, that determine the future chapters of our lives.

As I share some of the chapters from my life, may you experience hope, joy, laughter, and tears. Most important, however, be encouraged that the Author of your one life on earth wants to use you to make an impact on people for eternity.

Blinded
by the Light

As a junior in high school, I was seriously over-weight. It hadn't dawned on me yet that my body was God's temple, and that I was making His temple into my trash can.

It was prom season, and it seemed like everyone I knew had been invited to the junior prom—except me. I was desperate to get a date, but nobody would ask me. Even when I did the asking myself, no boy would accept. I ended up paying my friend's brother to take me—I even paid to rent his tux. Talk about humiliating!

I'd always loved flowers, and for my prom dress I bought a blue polyester floral print number to match my eye shadow. No one told me a print would make me look twice as big as I really was. And to make matters worse, I had the hardest time finding shoes in just the right shade of powder blue. I finally settled on a pair of blue plastic thongs from K-mart, which set me back ninety-nine cents.

As I was posing for my photo at the prom, a guy I had a terrible crush on (not my date) came up to me and said, "Sheri, are you going to the beach?" which I thought was his way of asking whether I was going to party on the beach after the prom. Maybe he would invite me! "Why, are you?" I asked. "No," he shot back with a satisfied smirk. "I just thought you were going to the beach because you look like a whale, and you're wearing thongs!"

I didn't see how my life could get any worse. But that was before somebody put LSD into my drink at my sixteenth birthday party. This unexpected surprise resulted in a three-day "trip" filled with hallucinations—bugs on the walls, evil faces on the ceiling, and a horrifying feeling that I was floating uncontrollably through the air.

I have no idea how I got home. When I finally came to, I was on the bathroom floor in my house, crying hysterically. My stepmom, Susie, cautiously opened the door to see what was going on. I ran into her arms and cried,

"I hate my life! Please help me!" So many times in the past I had run away from her advice and love. Though I didn't understand it at the time, God prepared my heart to run to *her* and admit I was lost and afraid and needed her guidance.

She agreed to help, but only under her conditions. I had to give up the rebellious lifestyle I had gotten comfortable with—wild weekends, sugar fixes, drugs, cigarettes—everything. I was so desperate I was willing to give it a try.

When I got back to school, the party rumors had gotten to class before I did. My English teacher walked right up to my desk, pointed her finger in my face, and sneered in slow, deliberate tones, "Sheri Rose, you will *never* amount to anything." Her condemning voice echoed off the chalkboards, accompanied by the snickers of two dozen teens.

I was devastated. Fortunately, my English teacher wasn't in charge of the grammar lesson for life. Can't you just hear God saying, "Don't put a period where I have a comma because I have a plan for every life I create."

I didn't know God then, but by the time I was graduated from high school I had lost fifty pounds and kicked my drug habit. I decided to enter my first beauty pageant, Miss San Jose–California.

Talking with other contestants backstage the night of the competition, it soon became painfully obvious to me that nobody else had experienced the kind of life I had. I began to wonder who would want damaged goods like me as a public role model. An ex-druggie in a beauty pageant? From a broken home? No way.

My self-confidence was headed downward in a death spiral when my dad walked up to me, looked deep into my eyes, and said, "Sheri, I'm so proud of you for what you've accomplished with your life." There is incredible power in a parent's encouragement. His few words changed my whole outlook. (If you're a parent, take a moment to encourage your children today. They need your love and support more than you can imagine. A few positive words only take a moment, but that moment will turn words into beautiful melodies that will echo in their ears for a lifetime.)

After my dad's encouragement, I was ready to give those judges a performance they would never forget. I thought I was totally prepared, complete with briefings on current events, modeling classes, and speech training. My dad, the king of trade-offs, even gave a plastic surgeon a trip to Maui so I could get a new nose.

Part of every pageant is when contestants do "the walk," parading one at a time down a runway toward the audience. The runway and stage are lined with tiny lights, and spotlights follow the contestants like a movie star as they walk, dressed in evening gowns, down to the end of the runway, make a turn, and walk back.

Of course, during rehearsal, we had all practiced smiling, waving, and walking at the same time, and plenty of us had done it since we were children. During the rehearsal, however, there weren't a thousand people sitting out in the audience, and the Miss San Jose crown was not actually on the line like it is when contestants are doing the walk in the live event. An even bigger difference is that during the competition, the auditorium is pitch dark, the spotlights are right in their eyes, and they can't see a thing in front of them—even if the thing in front happens to be a table full of judges.

When my turn came, I sauntered confidently down the runway toward the light, beaming my best competition smile and doing the figure-eight wave like a pro. I took one step after another until suddenly, there was nothing to step on. I went flying through space off the end of the runway and landed with an unqueenly thud smack in the middle of the judges' table.

The audience gasped in unison. All was lost. But just because I was flat on my face didn't mean I couldn't be quick on my feet. Mustering my perkiest smile, I rolled off the judges' table and hopped up on my heels. I then straightened my sequins, looked up at the judges without missing a beat, and exclaimed, "I just wanted you to remember me." And with that, I crawled back onto the runway and walked offstage the right way. If I was going to go down in flames, I might as well go with a little panache.

I learned a reliable lesson that night. It's *not* how I act; it's how I react that makes the difference. They not only remembered me, they awarded me the title of Miss San Jose. It was a case where tragedy turned into victory (though I don't recommend it as a strategy for aspiring pageant contestants).

From embarrassment to triumph! How many peaks and valleys could there be in one day? After my victory, my family and I all went to a Mexican restaurant to celebrate. I was starving! I hadn't eaten real food in three weeks. With admiring relatives and curious onlookers surrounding me, I lunged for the nachos, and my shiny new crown slid off and scored a direct hit into the refried beans. God never runs out of imaginative ways to keep us humble.

Pumped Up

After I won my very first beauty pageant, I couldn't wait to put on my crown and banner to make my first public appearance (my first appearance, that is, after washing the refried beans out of my crown). Even though I was only Miss San Jose, I felt like Miss Universe.

A few weeks after my victory I was scheduled to ride in a parade. I would get to sit in a convertible and do that little figure-eight wave for three hours while staring at the backsides of forty-two overfed horses. Driving to where the parade was supposed to start, I noticed that my brother had neglected, as was his habit, to fill up the gas tank.

I was running at least fifteen minutes behind schedule, as was my habit. The last thing I wanted to do was stop for gas, but I had no choice. Fully decked out in my crown and evening gown, I pulled into a service station as quickly as I could. This was in the pre-self-serve era, and I hollered to the attendant, "Please fill up my tank as quickly as possible. I have to get to a parade!"

He scurried around the back of the car and then came to the window and took my money. I assumed that he was done pumping the gas, so I flew off as quickly as I could because I had no intention of being left out of my first parade. As I was driving, I noticed people in their cars waving at me and pointing. *How sweet*, I thought. *My adoring fans recognize me as the new Miss San Jose. This beauty pageant gig is even better than I expected.*

Then a man pulled up next to me, and he did not have the expression of an adoring fan on his face. It was more an expression of exasperation mixed with a touch of rage. I was driving as fast as I could and honestly had no time to stop for autographs or photos with the family. *If it's that important*, I thought, *he'll just have to follow me to the parade. I'll be happy to give him an autograph then.*

At last, the parade! I screeched to a halt, leapt gracefully from the car, and ran over to find my place.

Suddenly this man came driving up behind me. He jumped out and sprinted toward me as fast as he could. This guy was really desperate. At first I couldn't understand what he was shouting, but it sounded a lot like, "Give me my gas pump back!" No wonder he was steamed. I had driven off and ripped the nozzle and hose right off the gas pump. There they were, trailing along behind me like a big rubber tail. Oops!

I didn't know what to say. Then I remembered I was, after all, Miss San Jose, so I asked in all earnestness, "Can I give you an autographed picture? Will that help? Can I mention your gas station in my speech? Is there anything else I can do?"

"Yes," he said. "You can pay to have my gas pump fixed."

It was an unforgettable demonstration to me of what happens when I'm too busy thinking about myself. I ended up setting a bad example, offending people, and looking extremely silly (not to mention possibly having to pay for a broken gas pump). Wonder what people thought about pageant winners after they saw me?

Dumped
On

Spending long summer days at the beach is the splendid stuff teenage dreams are made of . . . unless of course the teenager looks like I did in high school. Back then, the only thing grander than my humiliation was the size of my swimsuit.

I had grown up in California where slim, toned, and tan people strut around confidently in bathing suits all the time, and where I never appeared in public without a coverup or some other form of camouflage that would hide my "Sheri the Whale" silhouette. So when I finally lost fifty pounds during my senior year, I was elated about being thin and able to show off my new body in a swimsuit. (Keep in mind this was before I became a Christian.)

It was time for my coming-out party.

A national volleyball tournament was going to be held on the beach, and I was determined to make a good impression . . . and maybe a few dates. In a big way, I was going to make up for all those fat jokes and lost time! I knew there would be national media coverage of the tournament and that sports agents and casting directors would be looking for new talent. I was determined to get the attention I'd always longed for.

I arrived at the beach tournament in a white swimsuit, with a white towel, white sunglasses, white hat with little white sandals to match, a white fold-out chair, big rhinestone earrings, my makeup on perfectly, and my hair freshly styled. I made a royal entrance, flashing my best beauty pageant smile and parting the sea of wide-eyed weekend wayfarers with my radiantly white ensemble. Despite the urge, I refrained from doing my little wave.

Everybody was looking at me. I didn't care that I was the only person on the beach who looked like she had been getting dressed to attend a formal dinner and then suddenly decided to go watch a volleyball game instead. I imagined a scuffle breaking out among the casting directors to see who could get to me first. They were no doubt assuring each other, "She's obviously the next Hollywood megastar."

Thousands of people had gathered for the tournament. Thousands of people mean lots of food. In southern California lots of food mean lots of seagulls—flocks and swarms of seagulls. And we all know what lots of seagulls eating lots of food eventually generate.

My elegant and perfectly positioned hat was too tempting a target to pass up. Of all the people they could have chosen to unload upon, the seagull bombardiers chose the one in dazzling white who was busily making a lasting impression. Little did their target know how lasting her impression was soon to become.

My ensemble had attracted plenty of admiring onlookers, but no one was watching the sky as an enemy seagull opened the bomb bay doors high overhead. In other words, all eyes were on me when a big (and I mean humongous) blob of seagull poop landed— splurff—on the edge of my hat. With an impeccable sense of timing, it lingered briefly on the brim before proceeding to drip into my perfectly styled hair.

Summoning what shred of poise I could, I removed my hat (carefully), cleaned up my hair and hat with my towel, and wished I could sink beneath the sand without a trace. My regal aura was shattered. I definitely got the attention of an adoring audience. All eyes were on me, all mouths were laughing, and all fingers were pointing. What a mess I was a part of! Literally.

The Word of God says, "Humble yourselves before the Lord, and he will lift you up" (James 4:10, NIV). At that time in my life I was too busy lifting up Sheri Rose to pay any attention to God. My big day at the beach was an unforgettable lesson in humility. When we try to exalt ourselves above others, we set ourselves up to be dumped on. To make this point clear, God will use whatever it takes—dive-bombing seagulls included.

Cleaning Up Friendships

When I was in high school, a friend of mine was going through some tough times at home, and I wanted to help her. I went to her home one afternoon to see if there was anything I could do. It was quickly obvious that the house hadn't been cleaned in months, so I decided I would take the initiative and tidy things up a little while my friend's mother was out.

Then, as now, I was not very adept at cleaning house. I was from the kick-it-under-the-couch-or-hide-it-in-the-fridge school of home economics and honestly had no business cleaning up someone else's belongings considering the condition of my own. (To this day there is an unspoken rule in our house that after I make dinner, I hand the apron to Steve, who graciously restores our disheveled kitchen. After all, cleaning is not my gift, and we should all avoid trying to operate outside our gifts, don't you think?)

Nonetheless, spurred on by teenage enthusiasm, I decided to surprise my friend's mother and clean up her house. I vacuumed the rugs, dusted everything that didn't move, and even gave the bathrooms a going-over. I was feeling pretty smug as I sailed into the kitchen. I'd saved the worst for last. There was food sitting on the counter that had been there a long time, growing green fuzzy stuff. I filled the sink with hot water and got to work.

While I was on a roll, I decided I might as well go ahead and clean out the refrigerator. On one shelf after another, an extended family of those green fuzzies had taken up residence. Another week and they may have started answering the phone.

I pulled dishes out of the refrigerator with gook on them old enough to interest the Smithsonian. Clearly this was the sort of toxic waste that was beyond the scope of soap and water. I felt like it would be, well, too hard to actually wash these dishes or even soak them. Obviously they couldn't be worth anything to anybody and were probably garage sale rejects just taking up space. The house had been such a mess, I figured no one would notice if I threw dishes and all into the trash.

I must admit that, as much as I enjoy helping others, I also enjoy their reaction to my efforts—the smiles, the thanks, the heartfelt words of gratitude. I stayed with mounting excitement, watching television and waiting for my friend's mother to get home. I had cleaned and reorganized her entire home—she was bound to be delighted!

I heard her coming in through the kitchen. The footsteps stopped. Silence. *She's looking around in astonished admiration,* I thought with a grin. Then I heard it—a wretched, horrid, heartrending scream at the top of her lungs. I came running in shouting, "What's wrong? What's wrong?" She looked at me, with lips quivering and veins bulging, and gasped, "Somebody threw out my grandmother's china!"

I realized "somebody" had made a terrible mistake, and I began helping her fish the food-encrusted plates out of the garbage. Still, I couldn't help thinking that if this china was so precious to her, why did she allow dried food to sit on it for eons in the refrigerator?

My friend's mother treated her possessions like they had no value, so I thought they were worthless. The experience taught me that if something in my life is precious, I need to treat it accordingly. Other people will notice how I talk to my husband, how I discipline my son, how I nurture friendships and business associates, and may take their cues from me.

If I let those relationships grow green fuzzies, I'm telling the world they don't matter. If I keep them fresh, it shows they're important in my life. All in all, it's easier than keeping up with leftovers—and much more rewarding.

An Angel
in Slippers

When I was single, I had an argument with a boyfriend—not a little argument, but a giant economy-size argument. One night, weeks after our fight, I decided at about two o'clock in the morning that I had to tape a letter to his door *right then*. I went into the other bedroom in my apartment where Joyce, my roommate and best friend, was snuggled up asleep under a fluffy down comforter. She looked so snug and peaceful, but this was an emergency.

I sat down on the side of her bed. "Joyce?"

"Mmmmfph?"

"Joyce, could you please go with me to tape this letter on my boyfriend's door because I don't want to drive at night by myself?"

She opened one eye and said, "Sheri, just wait until the morning and I'll go with you."

"Please, Joyce, I have to do it now."

"Why do we have to do it in the middle of the night?"

"I can't sleep."

"Thanks to you, neither can I. What are the chances of you leaving me alone unless I say yes?"

"Slim to none."

"Thought so."

She got up, put on her robe and slippers, and marched down the stairs to get into my car I started to thank her for this wonderful sacrifice of a night's sleep.

"Just drive," she ordered.

I drove.

We got to my boyfriend's house, and I started taping the letter to the front door. He heard me and came outside. We hadn't spoken in weeks, so it was an awkward moment, not counting the fact that it was now about 3:30 A.M. He read the letter while I stood there and then invited me to come in and talk about it.

"Well, OK," I answered. "But only for a minute."

As we talked inside, I felt so relieved that our friendship was being reconciled that I completely forgot Joyce was still in the car in her early morning attire.

Now you might be wondering why Joyce didn't just come knock on the door and say, "Let's go home." Well, a Doberman pinscher had taken care of that. The minute I walked inside, the Doberman that belonged to the policeman living next door came charging over to the half-open car windows to have my best friend for a late-night snack. She couldn't roll the windows up because they were electric, and I had the key. She couldn't honk because my horn was broken. All she could do was sit there frozen in fear, just like a deer caught in headlights—only with slippers on.

After what seemed like only a few minutes, my boyfriend and I had worked everything out. It wasn't until he opened the front door—and I saw my car with a bare-fanged Doberman snout poked in as far as it would go—that I remembered I had left Joyce in the car. I looked at my watch. She had been sitting there, inches from being a doggie treat—for three hours!

My boyfriend could not believe it. "I've heard of leaving your keys in your car," he quipped, "but your best friend?" As he shooed his neighbor's pooch back home, I got in the car and begged Joyce to forgive me. Fortunately, she was too tired to be really mad. All she wanted to do was pick up where she'd left off under that fluffy down comforter.

After we got home and I finally got into bed, I started thinking about how easy it is to miss some of God's greatest gifts because we just aren't paying attention. As I lay there, the night's little adventure was only one of a dozen examples I could recall that reminded me how important Joyce's friendship was. Obviously, God brought her into my life for a very special reason. And here I'd abandoned her to the robe-devouring wildlife of suburbia—too focused on my problems and too forgetful of my blessings.

When we're going through problems in our lives, it's easy to get so wrapped up in ourselves that we overlook the "Joyces" that God brings along to bless us, minister to us, and help us through. We ask for help, then ignore it when He puts the answer right in front of our noses—or a Doberman's.

The Greatest
Crown of All

When I was twenty-four, I was nominated as one of America's Most Outstanding Young Women. I'd gotten off drugs, become a successful businesswoman, had plenty of boyfriends, and made plenty of money. But behind closed doors, this outstanding young woman was throwing up my food seven or eight times a day and crying myself to sleep almost every night, just like I did in high school when I smoked marijuana and was fifty pounds overweight.

It was a private hell I couldn't tell anyone about. What right did I have to complain? By the world's standards I had everything. To me, though, I was living a lie. I couldn't continue pretending I was a perfect person, and no amount of money or beauty pageant crowns or boyfriends could help me.

Eventually I got so depressed that I thought about taking a handful of sleeping pills and ending my sad, miserable life. One night I ate a whole tray of desserts, threw them up in the bathroom, then fell on my knees in the bedroom, crying hysterically. I grabbed the bottle of pills and held it in my hands. What was there to live for?

I threw myself to the floor and closed my eyes. I had a flashback, recalling the face of a guy in high school who used to sell me drugs. Boy, was he messed up! Then one day somebody invited him to youth camp at a church. When he came back, he quit selling drugs, and went back to his neighborhood to hand out Bible literature, telling his old customers that Jesus was the answer to their cravings, not dope.

Then I saw the face of a man who bought me a tank of gas when I was stranded but wouldn't let me pay him for it. He handed me a Bible tract and said, "Read this for me instead. Jesus has a plan for your life."

Stretched out on the floor of my room, agonizing over what to do with my life, I cried out, "God, if You exist, please show me!" I fell asleep, still holding the un-opened bottle of sleeping pills.

I was awakened by the telephone. The sun was up, and I felt a peace and sense of relaxation I hadn't felt in years. The call was from a friend inviting me to have dinner with his grandparents. I accepted and soon found that his grandparents were missionaries in Romania.

Let me clue you in on a little secret. If missionaries start praying for you, you might as well give in and do whatever they're praying for you to do because it's going to happen anyway. As soon as they heard what had been happening in my life, they prayed that I would find my direction according to God's will.

Later in the evening, as I got ready to leave, I wished so much that I could stay there and enjoy the refuge and peace of their house. At that instant the grand-mother said, "Sheri Rose, how would you like to stay here with us while you're in town?" I jumped at the chance; I ended up spending almost a month with them, hearing the remarkable story of their work on the mission field.

They knew I had an interest in beauty pageants. Near the end of my stay, they asked if they could tell me about the greatest crown of all. "It's the crown of life, ap-pointed by God," they said, "and it comes with an in-credible prize package: a city of gold, a crystal sea, per-fect health, much happiness, and eternal life."

Sounded good to me. "How do I win this crown?" I asked eagerly.

"It's yours for free. There's no competition, and no one can ever take it away," they explained. "All you have to do is receive Jesus as your Savior and ask Him to forgive your sins. Ask Him to come into your life and give you the peace you're so desperately searching for. You won't find it any other way."

"I want to, but I'm scared," I admitted. "My Jewish family will turn away from me if I become a Christian."

They both put their arms around me. "When you're ready to surrender your life back to the One who gave you life, He'll be waiting for you."

In the weeks that followed I went back to producing showcases, back to bulimia, and back to black, frightening periods of depression. Surely I could handle this stuff somehow. Still, I found myself thinking more and more about this eternal crown. Could it be that simple? Just call on the name of Jesus and He will give me a new life?

I'd tried everything else, and none of it was bringing me happiness, contentment, or healing. At last, one night in desperation, I got down on my knees and prayed aloud, "Dear God, if Jesus really is Your Son, if He really is the way to heaven, and if calling on His name will really change my life, I'm ready. I accept Him as my Savior, and I repent of my sins."

I went to bed, but when I woke up the next morning, I had no urge to purge. I felt content, happy, and full of energy. That same afternoon, I was working out at the health club when two ladies approached me and asked if I was a Christian. "Um, I don't know," I mumbled. One of them was a minister's wife, and she invited me to her home for dinner. She and her husband offered to teach me more about God's Word, and I accepted gratefully. I guess God knew I needed accountability from the first moment I gave my life to Him.

Today, I know that the greatest crown of all is not a crown appointed by man, but the Crown of Life appointed by God.

I am thankful to be a daughter of the King!

A Few Good Men

Every woman dreams of the day she becomes engaged. My first engagement was tender and romantic and wonderful. So was my second. And my third! What made them even more memorable, however, was that they sort of, well, overlapped.

When I became a Christian at twenty-four, I was determined to marry a man who loved the Lord. I completely ignored the fact that I could pray for God to lead me to the right person, so I set off in search of "the man" on my own. To help God out, I decided to date every

Christian man I was attracted to. Since I was producing showcases and traveling so much, I could find a date in every city I visited. I got to know them over a period of time without either of us being too pressured. And, if one of them upset me, I had plenty of others to console me.

After almost two years of cross-country dating, I was confused and somewhat convicted that maybe this wasn't such a super idea after all. I even had a few dates with the fantastic Christian music artist Carman. He is a wonderful man, but he is too much like me. I once heard a pastor say that if a wife and her husband are exactly alike, there's a need for only one of them. Marry someone like me? Scary.

I finally realized my strategy wasn't working. I had given the rest of my life to God but not the all-important decision of whom I should marry. I had to wait on the Lord. I decided to take a break from the search and really pray to God for guidance. By that time, though, my eagerness to find a mate had gotten me into a mess.

Michael was a model who lived in Phoenix—a sweet college boy I had dated in the past, and we started seeing each other again. Although he was four years younger than I was, and not yet a Christian, he was one of the most fun and romantic men I'd ever met. When we renewed our relationship, I made it clear that I would be seeing other people and expected him to do the same.

One evening we were visiting a church, and Michael pulled out a ring and proposed. *Maybe this is a sign that he's the one,* I said to myself. After all, we were in church, and Michael always made me feel so special.

Looking back now, I see that my decision was based purely on emotion—not the least on faith or logic—but I said yes. After the service Michael promptly announced the news to a gathering of his friends. But telling a crowd was nothing compared to breaking the news to Dad.

Dad didn't hit the ceiling when I told him (he knew better). He just told me Michael and I were both in "La-La Land" and that our marriage would never last. I wouldn't budge. "Remember when you and Mom were going to get married, and everybody tried to talk you out of it?" I reminded him. "You didn't listen. You did what you thought was right."

"Yeah, and look how that turned out," he shot back, reminding me of my parents' nasty divorce that left scars on everybody in the family. "That's why I *know* it won't work for you, Sheri. It's history repeating itself. Please don't make the same mistake I did with your mom!"

He knew I wasn't listening, and that hurt his feelings. Eventually, he came to accept the idea of me marrying Michael. But about that time, I began having second thoughts. I had made the big decision. I had committed to this one man and fixed all my hopes on the idea that he, and no one else in the world, was the man I should spend the rest of my life with. I started feeling anxious and afraid. What if I made the wrong choice?

In the middle of the confusion, David, a chiropractor from San Diego I had been dating, called and invited me out to dinner. At the restaurant I kept trying to find the right moment to tell him I was now engaged to someone else, but David wasn't making it easy for me. He was the most fun he'd ever been on a date.

I kept trying to work the subject of my engagement into the conversation, yet as I sat there, my doubts about Michael were intensifying. I really did want a mature and stable man—security was important to me—and David was all those things. But I couldn't imagine sacrificing all the fun and romance I enjoyed with Michael.

Now tonight I was seeing a new side of David— laughing, funny, completely at ease. We were having so much fun! *What does this mean? Is David the one?*

Just as I was asking myself these questions, David reached into his pocket and pulled out an engagement ring. "I love you, Sheri, and I want to marry you," he confessed passionately.

My head was spinning. David had never said that he loved me before. "I've never told that to anyone before in my life," he said, as though he were reading my thoughts. "I've never used those words before because I only wanted to say 'I love you' to one person." I melted.

My mind was racing. *This must be God's way of rescuing me from marrying the wrong person!* I thought excitedly. *What else could it mean?*

So I said yes, leaving out the tiny detail that I was, in fact, already engaged. Surely God would work it out.

It was after one o'clock in the morning when I got home, but I had to call my wonderful stepmother, Susie. After I told her the whole story, there was a short pause on the line. "Sheri Rose," she scolded, "you're wasting your time with these guys. Carman is the one for you. How many times do I have to tell you that?"

"Carman's never around," I protested. "We see each other like every three months or something." But Susie stuck to her recommendation.

I was more confused than ever. Now I was engaged to two men at the same time. I prayed and puzzled over the situation, but I couldn't find the answer. During the next several days, Michael and David called me repeatedly on the phone, but I dodged their calls. I needed to get away from the stress and figure out what to do.

I remembered my friend Kyman, a carpenter in San Jose whose missionary grandparents were partly responsible for my turning to Jesus. Kyman had always accepted me unconditionally and never pressured, but there wasn't much "electricity" in our relationship.

I spent a blessedly relaxing week with Kyman and his grandparents. Kyman and I went to the beach, worked out together, and had dinner like we were the best of old friends. It was so relaxing and stress-free I never wanted our time together to end. I had been praying for God's guidance on this "men" thing, but instead of waiting for His answer, I decided to take charge of the situation again. (Am I a slow learner or what?)

One day out of the blue I said, "Kyman, let me ask you something. If I said I wanted to marry you, would you want to marry me?" I wasn't *asking,* of course. I was posing a purely theoretical sort of question, but Kyman missed the nuance entirely.

"Oh yes, Sheri," he said, his eyes welling with tears. "Yes."

Kyman was so easygoing and helpful (we *never* fought), and I loved his grandparents. "That's it!" I decided, momentarily ignoring the two other "its" in the equation.

I began plotting how to tell Michael and David that I was going to marry Kyman when I picked up the phone days later to hear a rich and familiar baritone. "How are you, Sheri?" It was Carman. He was calling to invite me to visit him in Tulsa.

I thought my brain was going to blow up. What was God trying to tell me now? Was He saying Susie was right all along? Was my proposal to Kyman yet another in a series of huge mistakes?

I said yes to Carman's Tulsa invitation but only if he promised to give me his undivided attention while I was there. (What I really needed was the undivided attention of a good therapist.) He agreed to my terms, and I flew out to meet him, leaving my three fiancés in blissful ignorance of each other, and of suitor number four.

I spent five days with Carman, and we had a wonderful time. He seemed to have all the qualities I loved in the other guys all rolled into one. I carefully avoided telling him that I was already engaged in triplicate. I phoned Susie. "I think you were right," I admitted to her. "I think he's the one."

On our last evening together, he said to me, "Sheri, I don't want to play any games. We both know why I asked you here."

I gulped. "What do you mean?"

"Well, we're both at an age when we're thinking about who we're going to settle down with, and you know I think you're very special. But . . ." He paused, searching for a word. My heart was pounding. "I'm in the middle of an unfinished relationship with someone else," he continued, "and I don't think it's right to start something new while something else isn't really over yet."

I started to cry, not because I was disappointed but because I felt daggers of guilt stabbing me right through the heart—three daggers, to be exact. Carman's love and respect for me had led him to be completely honest about his feelings, and here I was selfishly hiding the fact that I was engaged to three men at the same time.

"I just need to be alone tonight," I told him. I had to spend some time by myself to sort out all the confusion.

As Carman drove me to the airport the next day, neither of us said much. Once there, we hugged and said good-bye, and went our separate ways.

Back home, Susie rebuked me. "You're not trusting in God. Be patient. Have faith, and wait for Carman to finish with the others in his life."

"No, Susie," I said. "It's over."

I decided I needed to stage a talent showcase to take my mind off my troubles. After talking with my partner, Joyce, we decided to produce our next event in San Francisco.

Meanwhile, I still had been avoiding phone calls from Michael, David, and Kyman—all itching to get quite specific about the future. Susie had successfully kept them from finding out where I was.

Being industrious and in love, however, all three guys independently got the idea to do an end run around Susie and call my dad's office. Somehow each one got Dad to tell where I was. Once they learned which hotel in San Francisco I was staying in, I found myself the object of a three-way telephone ambush.

As each of them cornered me by phone, I stalled for time. I still thought anything would be better than the truth.

"I'm sorry, it's all just so overwhelming," I said to Michael (if he only knew how overwhelming!).

When David called, I told him, "Marriage is such a huge step, and I'm scared. I just need time to think."

"My parents have had a total of five divorces between them," I reminded Kyman, "and I don't want to follow in their footsteps."

They all asked to see me. "No," I told them, "I just need to be alone."

The talent showcase went smoothly, and finally the last night arrived. About 120 performers would be onstage during the show, and at the end of the evening winners would be announced. Just before the curtain went up, Joyce and I were talking to the performers backstage. I asked if anybody wanted me to pray for them. Several did, and I had just finished praying when Joyce walked over to me with a strange look on her face.

"You'll have to get down on your knees for this one," she whispered ominously. "Maybe even try fasting."

"What are you talking about?" I asked, knowing we had only sixty seconds until the curtain went up.

She led me to the curtain and opened it a tiny slit. "Take a look."

There was a big, happy, expectant crowd out there. "Great crowd," I observed.

"No, look down."

I looked down and saw all the talent judges in place and ready for the show. "Oh good, all the judges are here," I said. "Perfect."

"*No*," Joyce said with mounting alarm. "Look down there to the right in . . . the . . . first . . . row."

As the house lights started to dim, I focused on the spot. I looked down to where she pointed and thought I was hallucinating. Sitting side by side in the front row were Michael, David, and Kyman—my three fiancés, strangers to each other, lined up like birds on a fence.

Nothing in life could have prepared me for the sight of three men I had promised to marry showing up at the same time unannounced. I had to have a plan in a hurry. I cast my terrified-animal gaze at Joyce and whimpered pitifully, "You emcee the show. I'll stay back here." But Joyce wasn't buying.

"OK," I said, desperate for a compromise, "you go out and talk to them one at a time."

"That's impossible," she said. At least one of us was keeping her head. "There's no way I can talk to one of them without the others hearing."

The house lights were out. The music cue came. I had no choice but to start the show.

To say it was not one of my better performances would be a gross understatement. My hands were sweating. Perspiration trickled down my back, soaking my gown like a T-shirt after a workout. I had a nervous rash on my neck. My lips quivered, and I couldn't pronounce the names of the contestants or sponsors. I missed the cues others gave me and forgot to give cues to others.

As the end of the show drew near, I was so afraid of facing the consequences of my triple play that I started hyperventilating. Backstage I had to breathe into a paper bag to keep from passing out. My heart was pounding like a trip hammer, and my whole chest tightened until it hurt. *Maybe I'll have a heart attack,* I thought. *Then I won't have to face them!*

Onstage at the close of the show, I looked down at the front row to see all three men still smiling, thank heaven. But at that very moment, I saw Michael turn to the other two and say, "Isn't she gorgeous? That's the girl I'm going to marry." The smiles vanished as they began to compare notes. The show was over in more ways than one.

Before I could leave the stage, David shot me a furious look and stormed out, headed for the airport. Kyman, the quiet one, waited patiently in a corner. As I came out into the theater from backstage, Michael was in front of me in a heartbeat. Cornered, I had no choice but to come clean. "I'm so sorry," I told Michael as we ignored the audience, cast, and crew bustling around the auditorium. "I never meant to hurt anyone, but I can't marry you. I can't marry *anybody* right now. I should have been more honest. I truly do love you all, but trust me, you don't want to marry me either." Shocked into silence, Michael left in tears.

I told Kyman pretty much the same thing and left a message on David's voice mail for whenever he collected himself enough to listen to it. It sounds pretty cold, but I wanted him to hear my apology as soon as possible. I hung up the phone and stood there trying to collect my-self. How could I have hurt these men so? Why didn't I have the courage to be honest with them before some-thing like this happened?

Finally I got to the real question. Why hadn't I sincerely trusted the Lord to guide me in my dating relationships?

Joyce had gone up to our hotel room ahead of me and prepared a therapeutic bubble bath. She had also looked up passages in the Bible on God's forgiveness and written them on sticky notes posted all over the bathroom walls. Joyce was truly a gift from God—never judging, always loving unconditionally.

She had tried to warn me that this was a final frontier of my life that I was still trying to control. I had gone through the motions of praying for God to lead me to the right man, but I didn't have the will—the heartfelt de-sire—to turn everything over to Him. God had my atten-tion now, and I would make sure He didn't have to re-peat the lesson. Those few good men became three wiser men because they were smart enough to leave me!

I learned the hard way that honesty, even if it hurts, is better than the alternative—deception. Ultimately, the truth alone is the only thing that sets us free.

God Saved the Best for Last

After being engaged to three men at the same time, I decided to quit worrying about getting married and let God bring me the right man in His own time. Meanwhile, I discovered some long lost friends: chocolate, ice cream, cheeseburgers, fries, chips and dip, and other gastronomical delicacies. A year after my triple romance I had gained twenty-five pounds.

I was living in California by then, and one day Michael (one of the three ex-fiancés) called from Phoenix to say he had become a Christian and was going to be baptized. He wanted to know if I would come celebrate the occasion with him. This was a miracle. He hadn't been a Christian when I was dating him. How could I turn down an offer like that? So I flew to Phoenix, where Michael met me at the airport with his friend, Kevin.

Michael was obviously surprised to see my Body-by-Haagen-Dazs as I came out of the jetway, though he did his best to hide the shock. I had gone from best-in-swimsuit pageant contestant to thunder thighs—hard body to lard body. "Uhh . . . it's great to see you," Michael stammered. "We're headed for the health club. Bet you'd like to come along too, huh?"

I smiled but was not amused.

On the way to the health club we stopped by Kevin's house. As we walked inside I told myself this was all no big deal; I didn't *need* to be physically attractive. I was the same desirable person inside even if I was the heaviest I'd been since high school.

Then I walked inside and saw the Greek Adonis—well, Kevin's roommate, to be precise—talking on the phone. I had heard in passing that Steve was a model, an actor, and he was shooting a feature film with Keanu Reeves called *Bill and Ted's Excellent Adventure*. But nobody told me the important stuff. He was tall, blonde, muscular, and absolutely gorgeous.

Trying not to gawk and wishing my thighs had re-

48

tractable panels, I still managed to notice that he was talking about Jesus—sharing the gospel with an actress from the movie. In response to his glancing smile I said to myself, "Hmmmmm . . ."

The next instant I wondered whether I was headed for another ride on the same scary roller coaster. Was I being impulsive, or was this a splendid rush of providential insight? *Could this be the one?* I asked myself. *Maybe he likes heavy girls.*

Steve stayed on the phone the whole time we were in the house. Michael, Kevin, and I headed for the health club, where I began searching for the magic machine that would take off twenty pounds in ten minutes. Self-conscious and preoccupied, fumbling around with one of the weight machines, I looked up to see Steve walk in the door and straight over to me.

"You look like you need some help," he said, muscles rippling, his smile lighting up the room.

"I sure do," I wheezed, red-faced from trying to hold my stomach in. I was all thumbs and incredibly embarrassed. It was like I'd never been in a gym before. But I did learn something new—I can't push ten pounds up when I'm trying to suck twenty pounds in. What was it with me and men?

When I got back home, I continued to look for the Lord's guidance in prayer and Bible study. I also spent some serious time in the gym—just in case.

Steve and I started talking on the phone from time to time, and a few months later we discovered we were both going to be in Los Angeles on the same weekend. We agreed to meet, and my praying, Bible studying, and working out went into overdrive.

Our time together that weekend was peaceful and relaxing. Steve and I quickly became friends. I admired his heart for God so much. Girls fell all over him everywhere we went, but he told me he had made mistakes dating in the past. He had made a covenant with God not to date anyone until God made it clear that she was "the one" for him. He hadn't gone on a date in over a year. Now that's discipline.

The last night of our visit, while driving back from dinner, I knew I wanted to see Steve again. Putting on my best pageant runway smile, I turned to him and said, "Steve, I know you're planning on moving to Los Angeles this summer, but I sure could use your help as an emcee on my next showcase." I held my breath.

"Sure, I'd love to," he said after a moment.

"That's great," I said in my best matter-of-fact tone. But on the inside, the butterflies in my stomach were flying in formation, and I wanted to scream, *Yesssss!*

The showcase was in San Jose, and when Steve arrived I was in the middle of preparations and already exhausted. In no time he had the names of the contestants memorized, handled tons of details, and got plenty of attention from the girls. He was so focused on helping me produce a first-class event, he seemed not to notice his admirers in the slightest. He was everything I wasn't: calm, rational, detail-oriented, soft-spoken, and unaffected by the limelight.

After the showcase, Steve was anxious to get back to Phoenix where he and a friend were producing a play they had written. I had to act fast. That night Steve and I went on a long walk. I was still a baby Christian, and I loved to hear Steve sharing his knowledge about Christ and His forgiveness.

We also talked about the opportunity my showcases gave us to witness to aspiring actors. We both felt led to minister to them. By the end of the night, we had agreed to stage another showcase in Sacramento. That meant a whole month with my dream man!

When the time came for Steve to fly back for the Sacramento showcase, I headed for the airport to meet him in a sexy, form-fitting outfit. A pastor friend said I shouldn't be putting Steve through unnecessary temptation.

"*Unnecessary?*" I shot back. "This is *completely* necessary. I want him to want me." My hook was fully baited, and I had no intention of coming back empty-handed. (Let me repeat, I was a *baby* Christian at the time.)

To my astonishment, Steve's response to my knockout outfit was, "Say, you look really nice today."

I was crushed. The big one was going to get away. He did not adore me the way he was supposed to. He had not so much as held my hand, much less discussed dating. Marriage seemed the furthest thing from his mind—which made me love him all the more, of course.

In the following weeks, we worked on the showcase together. I still had a few weapons in my arsenal. I tried longer fake eyelashes, extra shots of perfume, and laughed harder at his jokes.

Something must have worked because we finally shared our first kiss. But Steve pulled back and encouraged us to remain friends, for the time being. I hated that. Just when I'd give anything for a guy to pull out a ring, he wants to be *friends!*

I tried the helpless routine, acting like I needed help in situations I could easily have handled myself. Steve was unimpressed: "If you want me to do something, all you have to do is ask." He was so honest and so unmoved by my womanly wiles, it was driving me stark-raving bananas.

It took a while, but I realized at last that the eyelashes and perfume were never going to do the trick. I had to call in the big guns. I had to give it all to God (finally it was beginning to sink in). I had to pray for God to move Steve's heart and bless our relationship.

It was hard to step out of the way. I'm often so engrossed in what I want that I end up elbowing God out of my life. It was time for me to sit back and let God do His work if He wanted Steve and me together.

With only a few days left before the end of the showcase, Steve took me to a quiet, elegant restaurant. I had told him that after the production was over, I was going to take a little time off and audit some courses at BIOLA (Bible Institute of Los Angeles in La Mirada) University. Suddenly, as though he had turned to a completely different script by mistake, Steve said, "How would you feel about me moving down to Orange County instead of up to L. A.? That way I could . . . well . . . be closer to you."

Even though I was sitting down, my knees started to knock. I excused myself from the table. Bolting into the ladies' room, I clutched the first unfortunate woman I met in a death grip and shrieked, "I met the man I'm going to marry and I think he's about to propose!" My innocent victim didn't seem to know whether to congratulate me or call 911. "Uh . . . we're all very happy for you, aren't we girls," she said calmly as she backed carefully out the door in case I had a sharp object concealed on my person.

When my knees settled down, I went back to the table. If Steve was serious about his acting career, it would be crazy for him to live that far from Los Angeles. He leaned forward over the table holding both my hands in his. "Well . . ." His customary composure was completely gone, and he was stammering like a schoolboy. "You know there's an excellent seminary at BIOLA, and

I've always wanted to continue my education." He paused. "Sheri, I've spent the last two years of my life feeling God is leading me to L. A., But the truth is, these last thirty days, God has showed me something totally different and incredibly better."

We both started crying at the same time. Steve put his finger to the pulse in his neck, laughing. "I'm so madly in love with you that my pulse is racing. Here, feel it." He guided my finger to the spot. ChuGUNG chuGUNG chuGUNG—it was pounding a mile a minute (about half as fast as mine).

When we got back to the hotel, Steve did something a little strange. He asked me to go into my room and pray for half an hour, seeking God's guidance and blessing on our relationship. I spent that unforgettable time flooded with emotions of thanksgiving and praise, praying that God's will and not mine would be done (particularly considering my will's track record).

Steve knocked at the door, smiled a mischievous smile, and led me by the hand down the hall to his room. On a small table in the middle of the room were three candles, two of them lit. We knelt facing each other across the table, our hands clasped.

"Have you ever had Communion?" he asked softly.

I had grown up in a Jewish home and was a relatively new Christian. I shook my head no, not daring to take my eyes off of Steve's.

He explained the significance of Jesus' sacrifice and how the Lord's Supper symbolized both that sacrifice and our covenant with God. Together we ate the bread and drank from the cup (a plastic one from the hotel). Steve then took both my hands, bowed his head, and prayed for God's guidance in our relationship and His blessing on our future together.

After the prayer our eyes met, and Steve asked me to marry him. When he asked, I knew the question came straight from the Lord. When I said yes, there was no hesitation, no doubt that this was God's will for my life. We lit the middle candle together, signifying the strength of two, ignited by the very Spirit of God.

When I got back to my room, I was so awed by what had happened and how God had answered my prayers. I wondered aloud, "Do I really get to keep him, Lord?"

Faith triumphed where false eyelashes had failed.

Farm Fashions

Rather than tell his family when we got engaged, Steve decided to spring me as a surprise at his grandparents' fiftieth wedding anniversary. A big celebration was going to be held at Steve's uncle's farm in North Dakota, so we went up to join in the festivities.

It was the first time I would meet my future in-laws. I was determined to look my best. I had long since forgotten the lesson I learned at the beach volleyball tournament a few years before. Having grown up in southern

California, my mental image of a "farm" was the palatial country estate from *Dallas,* complete with Mercedes convertible, elegant dinner parties, radiant people, servants, private jets, and all the other necessities of life.

I dressed for the part accordingly. When Steve and I met at the airport, I was wearing a designer fleece jumpsuit embroidered with rhinestones, rhinestone earrings and jewelry, silver high heels, killer hair and nails, and the maximum amount of makeup allowed by law. Bobby Ewing would have fallen right off his horse. I figured if I could drive the airport metal detectors into a frenzy, I could make an unforgettable impression on Steve's family.

But Steve just stood there with a vacant look in his eyes. "Uh, it's very nice, honey, but I did mention that we're going to a farm, right? F-A-R-M?"

"Oh sure! I can't wait to meet everyone!" I gushed, completely missing the not-so-subtle hint.

Steve tried again. "Ummm, I'm not sure you're going to be comfortable in that, especially since we have to ride in the back of a truck for two hours after we get to Bismarck."

Steve's sister, Susan, strolled up then, dressed in jeans and a T-shirt. She gave me a quick look and said, "You look like you walked off the cover of *Vogue* magazine or something. You're going to a farm, you know." Then she belched.

Being the people-pleasing type that I am, I made a mental note, *Rhinestones are out. Belches are in.* I slithered meekly into the nearest ladies' room to change into something that was a little less dazzling without being completely frumpy. I emerged moments later in a peach sweatsuit with matching tennis shoes.

"Much better," Susan observed, and politely refrained from rolling her eyes.

I'm sure I was still quite a shock to the rest of Steve's family, but from the minute I arrived at the farm they welcomed me as one of their own. They weren't the least bit interested in whether my tennis shoes matched my sweatsuit. In fact, I bet they didn't even notice.

It was an important reminder that what's in our hearts is a lot more important than what's in our closets.

Come to think of it, Ruth didn't get her future husband's attention in the Bible until she rolled up her sleeves and toughed it out on the farm. Her simple devotion, faithful perseverance, and hard work landed her a place in history's honor roll as King David's great-grandmother, of the lineage of the Messiah, Jesus.

Target
Assumptions

When Steve and I were newlyweds, it didn't take long to discover we had different assumptions about life. About three days into our marriage, I asked if we could go to Target and pick up a few things for the house. Eager to please his new bride, he promptly declared it was a great idea.

It was there, among the aisles of jogging suits and tape players, that we learned just how different we were in this particular instance. His idea of picking up a "few things for the house" turned out to be the purchase of a jumbo-size package of napkins, paper plates, and some Windex. My idea of a "few things" was more on the order of a CD player, a wall unit, several sets of towels, shower curtains, decorator pillows for the bed, and his and hers matching desks.

As I was loading up my second shopping cart, my husband, who went faithfully to the gym several times a week, showed signs of hyperventilating. He thought he had married a Miss Practical Homebody, and here, among the washcloths and bath mats, he had a rude awakening. Actually, I *was* Miss Homebody—I wanted everything in the home section of Target in my home around my body. The grand total: three carts, $750, and a husband with heart palpitations.

Further discoveries about our different assumptions awaited us at home. I hung up our new hand towels in the bathroom and said, "Steve, honey, you are not to use these towels. They are just for decoration." Ever practical, my husband of three days said, "If that is the case, why don't you just take a picture of the towels and hang that on the wall?"

Having had his say, Steve walked into the bedroom and collapsed onto the pile of new decorator pillows. "Aaarghhh!" I yelled, snatching them out from under him in horror. "You can't lay on these! These pillows are just for decoration."

My definition of a cozy home was having rooms that looked like they were posing for *House Beautiful,* and no one had ever set foot in them. His idea of a cozy home was for everything in the house to have a practical purpose— why buy it if it's not good for anything? Not only had my poor husband spent $750 on doo-dads; he wasn't even supposed to use them. He just couldn't understand that.

On the issue of interior decor (and on other issues from time to time), each of us assumed the other thought the same way we did. When we discovered our differences, we didn't celebrate them and learn to accommodate each other; we got huffy. I doubt God put us together for that. I like to think we learned our lesson, and compromise now instead of snipping at each other. Sometimes.

The Amazing
Disappearing Cake

I love to eat. For someone with a passion for fine cuisine, what greater job could one have than that of a highly-paid food critic? Well, as a teenager, I was fortunate to land such a dream job. No, I didn't work for *Bon Appétit*. I was (don't laugh) a food spy for der Wernerschnitzel. My secret mission (for which I was more than compensated) was to chomp on chili cheese dogs, french fries, and apple turnovers at various store locations and then rate the cuisine and the service for the commandants back at HQ.

No one pays me to eat anymore, but that hasn't slowed me down. Sometimes food is all I can think about. When a meeting or even a wedding ceremony lasts more than a few minutes, I find my mind wandering in the direction of the buffet table. What will there be to eat? How much chocolate? I *run* to cake-cutting ceremonies to make sure I get a corner piece with lots of frosting. Buffets are particularly wonderful because they put the desserts out first. Sweets are the true nectar in the food chain of life. No wonder they're at the top of the government's new food pyramid.

When Steve and I first got married, we read somewhere that sugar can cause depression, weaken the immune system, and zap energy. So we made a commitment that we would not eat sugar for the first month of our marriage. Steve had the discipline to withstand the siren call of cookies and candy in the house, but I soon realized that if there was sugar in the house, I would snarf it down without a second thought. We decided not to keep desserts or sugar in the house for a whole month.

A sugar-free month was going to be tough. I began casting covetous eyes at toddlers who carried Twinkies past our apartment. Then I remembered the top of our wedding cake in the freezer waiting for our first anniversary! It was beautiful, elegant, and terribly alone. I knew the taste of its rich cream cheese frosting and moist, satisfying carrot cake innards. During the day, when Steve was at seminary, I began thinking about that lonesome, delicious cake. What could one little taste hurt?

Then I thought how disappointed Steve would be to discover he'd married a devious, ungodly woman who was not strong enough to keep her word. I couldn't let him see that I had cut a slice out of the cake. What if I just unwrapped it and looked at it and maybe smelled it a little bit? What could that hurt?

I got the cake out of the freezer and carefully took the aluminum foil off. There it sat on the kitchen counter in all its splendor, more beautiful and fragrant and desirable than I had remembered.

Without my telling it to, my finger raked itself lightly across the icing and stuck itself in my mouth. I savored the cold, buttery cream cheese, and by the time I overcame this distraction, my finger had made its cake-to-mouth round-trip two or three times. Shocked and dismayed, I grabbed a spatula to repair the damage, working carefully because the cold had made the icing brittle.

After a minute I was relieved to see that I had hidden all traces of my finger's rude behavior. With the icing back in place, no one would ever know the cake had been touched.

Click!

A little light went on in my head. If I didn't mess up the icing, Steve would never know I had broken my no-sugar promise. Carefully I tilted the cake over, cut several thin slivers out of the bottom with a knife, wrapped it back up, and put it back in its spot. As Laurel and Hardy used to say, "No one will be *any* the *wiser.*"

That night Steve never expected a thing. He wasn't likely to unwrap the cake anyway, but even if he did, it would look absolutely pristine. "My goodness, what an honorable wife I've been blessed with," I could almost hear him saying. From then on, whenever I needed a little sugar fix—say once or twice a day—I expertly unwrapped the cake, dug out more of the bottom, then wrapped it back up. If Steve was studying at home when I needed a taste, I made loud, distracting noises so he'd leave and go to the library.

Everything went well for a week or two, until one Saturday when Steve opened the freezer and started rearranging things to get a couple of steaks out of the back. A box of frozen peas fell on the cake-shaped foil, which was by that time an empty shell of cream cheese icing, and crumpled it on impact into a shapeless blob. Unwrapping the mess, Steve discovered my crime (just as the Bible warned would happen—"Be sure your sin will find you out" [Num. 32:23, KJV]).

He was compassionate and understanding; I was mortified and ashamed. I asked his forgiveness, and he gave it generously. To patch things up, we went out for ice cream since there wasn't any in the house.

Lose the Battle, Win the War

Growing up, I was quite bitter and resentful toward my mother. I didn't understand why she couldn't express love in a language I could understand. I didn't know why she wouldn't listen to me. I didn't know why she couldn't tuck me in at night. I didn't know why she was always comparing me—unfavorably—to my friends.

Now I know that my mother was only teaching me what she had learned herself. She was raised in an abusive home where no one showed her love, and she never learned how to love others or to express love. As an adult I grew to understand that she loved me to the best of her ability, but she was emotionally paralyzed.

When I became pregnant, I wanted to make things right with my mother. I had done a lot of things to hurt her because of my bitterness, and she had done a lot to hurt me. I felt it was time for a truce and reconciliation. I could benefit from her experience with newborns, and the baby would give us an incentive to rebuild our relationship. I was determined to make things right with her before the baby was born.

While I was working toward my decision, my mother made a decision of her own. One day I got a box from her in the mail. Anticipating a gift for the new arrival, I opened it to find my baby shoes and all my baby pictures. Also inside was a letter from my mother telling me how much I had hurt her and she wished I had never been born.

Well, if you've ever been pregnant, you know that even diaper commercials can turn you into an emotional wreck. Needless to say, after this "care" package, I was crushed. Devastated. I needed a serious talk with the Lord. "Lord," I prayed, "how can I forgive this woman? How can I make things right? I feel like I didn't do anything wrong. It's not my fault that she was abused growing up."

In the midst of my little pity party, I felt the Lord say in my spirit, *I didn't do anything wrong either, but I went to the cross for you. Don't try and forgive your mother in your own strength. Forgive her because you love Me.*

Out of obedience to God, I wrote my mother a letter asking her forgiveness for everything I had done to hurt her. It was the beginning of a miraculous change in our relationship. Today my mother is a Christian, and God has reconciled our relationship. Today we love one another and have the relationship I longed for over so many years. If only I'd gone to God sooner!

It was only after I was willing to admit I was wrong that the healing could begin. I had to lose the battle to win the spiritual war. If there is someone in your life you don't think you can ever forgive, remember that to forgive is to set a prisoner free.

Once you do it, you'll realize that the prisoner was you.

Tahoe Fever

When we got married in the fall of 1987, Steve and I were too busy with work, midterms, and other commitments to have a real honeymoon. That made me all the more excited as I anticipated a quiet week snuggling together at Lake Tahoe right after Christmas.

I arrived on the scene completely arrayed in designer ski wear, matching boots, earrings, and sunglasses, ready to hit the slopes. Unfortunately, instead of the time of my life, I had the nausea of my life. Some kind of bug was in there turning my insides to shredded wheat. Rather than schussing through the nine inches of fresh snow surrounding the lodge the next morning, I spent the day hustling back and forth between the lodge and the nearest ladies' room, fighting this mysterious Tahoe Fever.

By midday I had become a regular customer in stall number three. As I was making yet another visit to the cubicle of despair, I was startled to hear sounds similar to my own coming from the next stall. A few moments later, the other victim and I stood side by side at the sinks, rinsing and spitting with as much decorum as we could muster.

"You got the flu too?" I inquired compassionately.

"Nah," she responded with a voice of experience. "I'm pregnant again."

As we compared symptoms, I slowly came around to the realization that I may have been stricken with a severe case of pregnancy. After nobly offering to stay inside with me, Steve heeded my pleas for him to go out and do a little skiing by himself. I staggered outside into the crisp, bracing air to catch him at the end of his next run. As he skied in, I sprinted (sort of) to meet him. "Quick!" I said, without an extraneous or time-consuming introduction. "You've got to get me a pregnancy tester. Right now."

"Why would you think you need a pregnancy test?" he asked, all innocence and concern.

"Because I met a woman in the rest room who was throwing up, and she's pregnant!"

"That's not how you get pregnant, sweetheart. It isn't contagious." I failed to see the humor.

The test confirmed my acquaintance's diagnosis, and on the long ride home from Tahoe, I had time to sit and imagine what life would be like as a mother. Years before, I had made a checklist of all the things I wanted to accomplish before I held my first newborn in my arms. Of the twenty-odd goals I had written down, I had only managed to do one: get married.

Steve knew I wanted to be close to family, and with a new seminary opening up in Phoenix, we decided this would be a good time to move from California to Arizona, a change we had been discussing since our wedding. He was shocked that his California girl would be willing to move to Arizona in the summer, but I was all for it.

At first it didn't seem like it could really be 120 degrees. It was dry and breezy, and I was preoccupied with getting into the new house. But on the second day, I experienced desert life first-hand when my flip-flops melted on the driveway. The area was beautiful, and Scottsdale is a wonderful city. But being pregnant makes a woman hot anyway—another person and life-support gear are in there heating up the body—and I decided I must have been insane not to wait until fall. (If you've never been to Arizona in the summer, try this do-it-yourself simulation: plug in your blow dryer, turn it on high, and stick it in your mouth.)

As summer sizzled by, I often wondered how I could possibly become the mother our child would need. We hadn't planned to have a baby so soon. We had taken all the right precautions, yet here we were on the verge of parenthood, ready or not. God had ordained that it was time to have a new life in our family, and I could only pray that He would give me the skills for the job. There was nowhere else I could get them from.

Finally the big day came. I went into labor, went to the hospital, and prepared myself to welcome a new Shepherd. Eight hours later, the little nipper was nowhere in sight. Sixteen hours went by, then twenty. Finally the doctor said, "OK now. Push, Sheri. Push. *Push!*"

"Me push?" I yelled back. "Why do I have to push? You're the one with the salad tongs! Why don't you just pull him out of there and get it over with?"

A few minutes later (by the grace of God and with very little cooperation from me), my beautiful, precious son, Jacob Andrew, was safely in my arms.

As we arrived home a couple of days later, Steve could sense my anxiety over the responsibilities of motherhood. "Just pretend you're baby-sitting," he suggested.

"But I've never baby-sat in my life!" I responded with mounting panic.

"That's all right," he said warmly. "Jacob's never had a mommy before, so you're both starting from scratch."

I breathed a quiet prayer of thanks for this wonderful man, and even put in a good word for the "Tahoe Fever" that had so enriched our lives.

Mirror, Mirror, Off the Wall

S teve and I can usually tell when something great is about to happen in our lives because it is preceded by an attack from the enemy. We both tend to be a teeny bit stubborn, which puts us on a collision course once we take opposite sides of an issue. One of our more memorable disagreements was the day before one of our productions in California.

If there's one thing I learned growing up, it was how to fight. I had watched my parents argue when I was growing up and listened from my room at night as they screamed at each other. These fights could last for hours—my dad red-faced, his carefully combed hair trembling in place like a little furry animal as he shook with fury; my mom's eyes wide and round like saucers and the veins in her neck sticking out. That kind of communication I could understand.

Poor Steve, however, was clueless. He was raised in quieter surroundings and had not had exposure to proper combat training. He obviously needed some lessons in losing his temper. He wouldn't fight, and his calm, reasoned responses made me even angrier.

Finally I'd had enough of this "let's work it out peacefully" stuff. He was only being nice to irritate me. "Why don't you show some emotion?" I screamed.

He stood there, calmly surveying my outburst. Suddenly he turned and released all that unhealthy pent-up tension by kicking the mirror on the closet door and smashing it to smithereens.

I was relieved. I could understand what he was saying.

Steve winced in pain. His big toenail jutted out at a bizarre angle. "Now if that's not enough emotion for you, I think I could probably work up a good cry."

Wow, I thought at the time, *what a performance. He sure learns fast.* I should have been more willing to learn, too, but I was too ready to argue. And at the time, there was nothing teachable in my spirit.

Why is it that doing the Christian thing seems so hard sometimes? The Bible says we all have hearts that are "desperately wicked," which means we'd rather look out for ourselves first than extend the hand of Christian mercy and forgiveness. Rather than teaching my husband how to fight, I should have followed his example and learned how to disagree without fighting. It was a missed opportunity that reminded me how precious Christian relationships are—and how foolish it is to waste them—not to mention expensive. It also cost me a pretty decent mirror.

A Message
Whose Time Has Come

Since I travel so much, I make it a point to take my little boy, Jacob, with me at least once a month. That way he gets to see what I do and hear my messages, and the people I visit always enjoy meeting him.

Once after he heard me share my testimony, including stories of my parents' stormy relationship, he started to cry because he said he was sad my mommy and daddy were too busy fighting to tuck me in. He said, "Mommy, I'm going to tuck you in bed for the rest of your life!"

Another time, he was with me on a Sunday morning when I spoke to a large church congregation. It was a gorgeous summer day, with sunlight flooding into the sanctuary, and I had felt especially blessed and anointed as I shared my testimony. I finished my message and was just getting ready to ask people to raise their hands and come forward if they wanted to give their lives to the Lord.

When, lo, I felt a tiny tugging on my elbow. I turned around, and there was little Jacob Andrew at my side in front of a church full of people. Thinking I could make this into a tender moment for everyone, my mind worked furiously on some pithy transition that used Jacob as a symbol for all who wanted to come forward and be trusting children in the eyes of Jesus.

I asked Jacob what he wanted. He crooked his little finger to have me bend down toward him. "I have to tell you a secret," he said.

Forgetting that I had a live microphone pinned to my lapel, I leaned down. In a ferocious stage whisper broadcast to every corner of the church, Jacob said, "Mommy, I have to go potty. And I have to go *now!*"

I always let people know that my first ministry is to my family. I was certainly able to provide an unforgettable example that day, leaving them standing at the altar for a brief bathroom break with my son!

Barbie
with a Bible

Onstage with the other finalists, I was so nervous I thought I'd hyperventilate. The master of ceremonies opened the envelope, paused for what seemed like an hour and a half, and announced, "Our new Mrs. United States of America is . . . Mrs. Arizona, Sheri Rose Shepherd!"

When I heard my name, I lost all the composure Mrs. United States is supposed to have. I screamed. I cried. My mascara ran until I looked like a punk rocker.

Somebody put a bouquet of roses in my arms, and cameras flashed from every direction.

As soon as I got backstage, Steve embraced me in a big bear hug. After all the struggles we had faced together, it seemed almost impossible that we were here. I've never felt God's presence closer than that night when, after years of difficulties and setbacks, we saw our lives transformed by His perfect will.

Steve and I had been staging modeling and acting showcases together since before we were married. These productions were a sort of "StarSearch" on the road. We got Hollywood agents and casting directors to come to a particular city, then put on a showcase to introduce them to the best talent in the area.

As well as coaching them on their performances, Steve and I used our showcases as a way to share Christ with young models and actors. They needed to know that, regardless of their poise or appearance, they were unworthy in the sight of God and were to seek His redeeming grace in their lives. (This goes completely against the grain of the show business mind-set—"look at me, I'm beautiful"—which makes being a Christian a special challenge in the industry.)

At the final dress rehearsal before each show, I shared my testimony, and Steve explained God's promise of salvation. Then we invited anyone who felt like it to pray with us. Almost everyone joined in praying for God to strengthen their faith and guide their lives.

For seven years we were on the road almost constantly, producing showcases all over the country. When our son, Jacob, was born, we packed him up with the lights and mixing consoles and brought him along too. I'm sure he thought everybody grew up riding around all day in airplanes and courtesy vans, eating out of disposable aluminum pie pans, and sleeping in a different hotel room every night.

I became pregnant again, and we started planning how to keep on with the shows even after I was home with a new baby. Those plans came to a devastating end a few weeks later when I had a miscarriage. I got pregnant once again but had another miscarriage. Steve and I tried to sort out God's will for our lives among so much sadness. We hardly had time to grieve, however, because we had to keep staging showcases to pay our production staff.

I was exhausted, but I continued working as much as I could. While sharing my testimony with a group of teenagers one afternoon, I blacked out and fell to the floor. I was diagnosed with chronic fatigue syndrome, and the doctors told me that unless I wanted to die young, I would have to slow down. I couldn't stand the thought of my little Jacob growing up without a mommy, so I spent my days on the couch, started gaining weight, and worried about how my forced retirement would affect our finances.

Steve was willing to continue producing the showcases and even staged one in Nashville without me. But it was not worth being separated from Jacob and me for weeks at a time. We agreed it would be better for him to look at some other career opportunities that didn't require so much travel, so he started pounding the pavement in search of a job that would put his contacts and skills to use.

As the bills began to pile up, Steve took jobs as a graphic designer, waiter, model, and limousine driver. But it wasn't enough to keep up with the cash requirements of our company. Finally, we had no choice but to declare bankruptcy.

On top of two miscarriages and chronic fatigue syndrome, it was almost more than I could stand. I was devastated, embarrassed, and wondered whether God was even on my side anymore. I had certainly tasted of His goodness in the past, but it seemed that the doors to everything in my life were all closing at once.

Eight months before all of this, I had agreed to produce the Mrs. Arizona Pageant, whose winner would go on to compete for the title of Mrs. United States. It was something I could do from our home in Phoenix, without traveling. However, I was so depressed by all the failures in my life that I felt I couldn't give the show the energy and attention it needed. I called the national pageant director and told her I couldn't do it after all. She would have to get another producer for her Arizona pageant.

Her response was a shocker. "No way! The pageant is in eight weeks, and you can't leave me without an Arizona contestant for the Mrs. United States telecast."

"I just can't," I explained. "I'm broke, too depressed, too tired, and there isn't enough time now."

Then, another shocker. "You've been in pageants before. You'll just have to represent Arizona yourself."

I said, "I am *not* in any condition—physically or emotionally—to compete in a beauty pageant. That was the old me. The new me is fat and tired."

She reminded me that I was legally responsible for turning up a Mrs. Arizona contestant. True, we had an agreement. If there was no Mrs. Arizona, I could be liable for the costs of the pageant. I had no choice but to agree to her terms.

I hung up the phone and dropped to my knees. "God, when I was little I always wanted to be a princess. Since I received the crown of life from You, I've never had any interest in a crown awarded by the world. In Psalm 37:4, the Bible says that I should delight in the Lord, and He will give me the desires of my heart. Could this possibly be Your will for my life?"

I had always dreamed of being a national pageant title holder, and here at last was my chance. There were, however, a few little details to take care of and not much time to do it in. First, I had twenty pounds worth of Twinkies and potato chips around my thighs I suddenly had to get rid of. Second, I was physically exhausted. Third, I had absolutely no pageant wardrobe—which would cost two or three thousand dollars—and I was absolutely broke. Steve and I got down on our knees that night and gave it to Him. If it was His will, He would provide.

The next morning I started trying to line up sponsors, fitness club memberships, and everything else I would have to have to compete. After less than thirty minutes on the phone, I had everything I needed. God had closed so many doors over the past few months, and now He was opening up a whole new series of opportunities, literally overnight. Like never before in my life, it became clear that God had built my faith by taking me *through* personal storms rather than *around* them. I learned that when God closes a door in my life, if I'd just get my face out of the way, it wouldn't hurt so bad.

In Las Vegas eight weeks later, I was crowned Mrs. United States 1994. As I stood there on the stage, crying with joy and shaking like a giant beaded baby rattle, I knew that God would use this platform for me to be a voice of hope to those hurting from a past life similar to mine.

I know some people see me and think, "Look, it's Barbie with a Bible. How can anybody who enters beauty pageants call herself a Christian?" This certainly was not my plan, but God's ways are not our ways. A crown and banner and a big bouquet of roses last only a moment. But I'm thankful for the opportunity to share my journey of faith and hope with thousands of people I would never have met if I had never won the Mrs. United States crown. God pulls all of us through rough times to prepare us for divine appointments in His service.

It doesn't matter where we start in life; it matters where we finish. God put us on earth to finish something. He never consults our past to determine our future. God loves us!

Remember not the former things,
nor consider the things of old.
Behold, I am doing a new thing;
now it springs forth, do you not perceive it?
I will make a way in the wilderness
and rivers in the desert.
Isaiah 43:18

Myrtle

P eople accuse me of having a fear of flying. That is not true. I don't have a fear of flying; I have a fear of crashing—which presents a problem since I get on an airplane almost every weekend. The night before I went to compete for the title of Mrs. United States, I had a panic attack. I told my husband that he would have to drive me to Las Vegas from our home in Phoenix because I was positive the plane was going to crash.

"Do you believe that God is sovereign?" he asked.

Isn't it maddening when a logical man gives a logical answer, but it is not the one being sought? We don't want them to *fix* it, we want them to *feel* it—"Of course I believe God is sovereign!" I then proceeded to dramatically explain that I knew he wanted me to die, or else he would get out of bed and drive me to Las Vegas.

When he absolutely refused to do this, I turned to the Lord in prayer. I went into my little boy's bedroom and knelt by his bed. "If Mommy dies," I intoned over his sleeping form, "don't let Daddy marry anybody else." You know, it was one of those selfless spiritual prayers.

The next morning Steve still insisted I fly to Las Vegas. On the airplane, steaming at my husband for sending me to certain death, I found myself seated next to an eighty-year-old woman named Myrtle. Myrtle was a charming lady who told me she was a Christian, and that she was writing a book about her life. I was immediately flooded with a sense of relief. *God's not going to allow this plane to crash,* I thought. *This woman has to finish her book.*

Myrtle was from Arkansas, and on the way to Las Vegas, she and I did what women do best: we spoke and listened simultaneously. We shared our life stories with each other, and when the plane finally landed, Myrtle told me I was going to win the pageant. She handed me her phone number. "Call me after you win so I can congratulate you."

I thought to myself, *Nice lady, but poor eyesight. And she hasn't seen me in a swimsuit.* (By the way, for those of you who don't know the difference between Miss America and Mrs. America, it's cellulite.)

I have absolutely no doubt that this wonderful woman was there by the providence of God to calm me down for the pageant competition when my own husband was not able to. The night I was crowned Mrs. United States, I had a long list of special people to call with the news. Myrtle was first.

Lying in bed late that night, dead tired, I looked over at my new crown sparkling in the moonlight. It occurred to me that it only glistened when light shone through it; it didn't have any light of its own. In the Sermon on the Mount, Jesus said for us to be the light of the world and the salt to the earth. It isn't a crown that makes a woman beautiful; it's the light of Jesus shining through her life that gives her a lasting beauty all will be drawn to.

I prayed that I would be able to reflect God's light into other people's lives—the way Myrtle brought light into mine.

Could I Have Your Autograph?

When I was a little girl, I dreamed that signing autographs would be the most glamorous thing in the world. Imagine—perfect strangers would want you to write your name for them!

It's not quite like that.

I do have the pleasure of signing lots of normal items like books, programs, and the occasional dinner napkin. But to my everlasting surprise, I have also signed hands, feet, foreheads, Band-aids, and towels. A lady once asked me to sign her baby's diaper (yes, it was clean) so she could give it to the little girl when she grew up.

I once had someone ask me to get up from the table at a banquet and go out to the car to pose for a picture with their show dogs—it would mean so much to the dogs. I did. Possibly the most unexpected fan encounter to date came when I was in the bathroom and a lady slid a picture of me under the stall. "Could you sign this before you get done," she hollered. "I don't have time to wait in line, but I want an autographed picture for my granddaughter."

Signing autographs also leads to memorable comments, such as the one from a little girl who came up to me with the sweetest face and asked, "Since you're Mrs. America, does that mean you're Miss America's mother?" Another girl even asked me if I sleep in my crown.

No, I don't sleep in my crown. The spikes would be murder. I don't clean toilets in my crown. I don't put on my banner, swimsuit, and heels to go to the mailbox. And I don't pick up Jacob after school in an evening gown doing the figure-eight wave. Most days I'm a wife and a mother; on weekdays I don't even style my hair or do my makeup. And when I don't wear makeup, I look like I don't have a face.

One particular day without makeup, I picked Jacob up from school in gray sweats and my hair in a bun. His teacher came with him to the car and said excitedly,

"This is so cute! Your little boy loves you so much that he actually believes you're Mrs. United States!"

With a big smile on my face I looked at her and said, "I am!"

With a look of incredulity she said, "You're kidding, right?"

Jacob was in kindergarten when I won the Mrs. United States title. At show-and-tell that week he had stood proudly in front of his class and said, "I want you all to know that my mommy is the new queen of the country."

That gave me a chuckle, but it's really sad when someone looks at us and says, "You're kidding—you're a Christian?" Whether we like it or not, the world is watching us to see what a Christian looks and acts like.

Let your light so shine before men, that they may see your good works and glorify your father in Heaven.
Matthew 5:16

One Lost Sheep

Almost every weekend I'm speaking in a different city. This has led to some incredible experiences, especially when my family comes along. We've been guests in some of the nicest hotels and most beautiful homes in the country, but one trip that really stands out is the one we took to a small town several hours away from where we live.

A group asked if I could come up with my family for a luncheon with about fifty ladies who they thought really needed encouragement. I felt led by God to meet with them, so my family and I decided to make a little vacation adventure out of it. We borrowed a van and brought a tent trailer with us.

We arrived at our hostess's hacienda, a beautiful estate on acres of property with horses and all types of animals, which our two-and-a-half-year-old son, Jacob, thought were absolutely fabulous. During a wonderful dinner, our hostess looked out of the window, saw our tent trailer, and suddenly exclaimed, "Oh praise God, you brought your tent trailer. We weren't sure what we were going to do with you because we really aren't comfortable letting strangers sleep in our home."

I thought, *What a great sense of humor. Imagine having a mansion with seventeen thousand bedrooms in the middle of nowhere and sending your invited guests outside to sleep.* Catching the spirit of the moment I said lightly, "Yeah, no problem! We can sleep on the lawn outside."

She said, "Oh good!" but sounded, I thought, a little too relieved.

I shot a furtive glance at Steve. We were beginning to get the picture.

We finished dessert and it was getting toward bedtime, but we were still at the table when our hostess said, "Are you guys ready to go out and go to bed? I'd like to go ahead and lock up the house."

I didn't want to make a bad impression in front of Jacob, so I said, "Sure, that'd be great!"

To which Jacob innocently responded, "Mommy, why are we sleeping outside? It's cold out there!"

Fighting my impulse to say, "Because this paranoid, stingy wench won't let us sleep in one of her bazillion bedrooms," I said instead, "We'll look at the beautiful stars! We'll get to sleep by the animals." And out we marched as the door locked behind us.

In the morning I was wondering if we'd have to wash in the horse trough when our hostess appeared at our campsite and said, "I wanted to be sure and invite you in to shower and get ready for the luncheon." Just when we started to think she wasn't gracious!

I came in, controlling my desire to suggest professional help, and tried to keep a good attitude as I dressed for the luncheon. When I sent Steve and Jacob inside to get ready, our hostess immediately escorted them back out to Camp Driveway. "I'm not going to be able to bring your family with us," she said. "They'll have to wait here. I hope you don't mind. Of course I can't let them wait in the house—you know how we feel about strangers in the house—but they can wait here at the property until we are done."

If you've ever been on a roller coaster so petrifying that you were too terrified to scream, you understand what our drive from the hacienda to the luncheon was like. We slowed to eighty for the curves, flying down skinny mountain roads with rocks on one side and sheer cliffs on the other. I shifted my travel praying into over-drive and hoped the angels could keep up with us.

Another surprise in a day of surprises awaited me. The luncheon organizers had forgotten to order a meal for their speaker, and there was evidently no way to cor-rect the oversight at this point. Just then a little voice in my head said, *I just want to point out, Sheri Rose, that you're* <u>*really*</u> *hungry right now.*

As I considered filching a roll or two off the head table, my hostess stood up, cleared her throat, and with the eloquence of an auctioneer, delivered a moving intro-duction with all of seven words: "Well, now it's time for our speaker."

I didn't respond to the cue fast enough. "Come on up! Hurry, hurry, hurry! We are all waiting to hear from you." Just then my stomach went "Aaaaurgggg!" I'm pretty sure it wasn't what she had in mind.

Why was I here? Why had I allowed this woman to treat me and my family like hired help with the measles? Could I gather my thoughts and make an effective pre-sentation after a night in a tent, a white-knuckle ride, an irritating separation from my family, no lunch, and the world's shortest intro? Well, the trip would certainly be something for the family scrapbook, and I knew deep down that a lesson in humility was never wasted on me. Since I believed God had called me here to deliver a message, I was determined to come through for Him.

The ladies had asked me to speak about encouragement. I talked about being an encouragement to others, and about forgiveness, and the freedom forgiveness brings to those who bestow it on others. Within minutes it was obvious that I had struck a nerve. Before I finished, there was not a dry eye in the audience. Many women in that room had been hurt and had been unwilling to forgive.

All of us came together as a group and forgave those who had hurt us. God's hand moved on one lady in particular. She had come with her children and hadn't spoken in years because she had been in such depression. Suddenly, she found freedom to forgive. Her kids were crying and hugging, and she was crying, and I was crying. It was amazing! Their family was reconciled on the spot.

Watching that joyous family, I couldn't help but think that Jesus loves us so much He would have gone to the cross for just one person. He cares that much about the one lost sheep. Earlier in the day, I thought I had made a miserable, pointless trip—but God knew better. By following His will in faith, I delivered a healing message to one of His lost sheep in a way I could never have anticipated.

Compared to the sight of that family literally dancing with delight at the forgiveness in their hearts, sleeping downwind from the barn wasn't so bad after all.

Finger
Food Follies

When I get hungry, I have to eat. I'm hypoglycemic, which means if I stay too hungry too long, my friendly Mrs. United States personality is suddenly transformed into something closely resembling a ravenous tyrannosaurus rex at a brontosaurus buffet.

On a trip to Washington, D.C., I was supposed to meet a disc jockey at my hotel and go to his radio station for an interview. But the person who picked me up at the airport took the wrong route, and I got to the hotel only a few minutes before I'd have to leave again for the broadcast.

I hadn't eaten since 6 A.M. It was already past lunchtime, and the interview would take another hour at least. With Mrs. United States and Mrs. T. rex fighting it out beneath my calm exterior, I called room service and said, "This is Mrs. United States. I have a radio interview in fifteen minutes. I am hypoglycemic and could really use some food *now*." I should note that this was not the kind of hotel coffee shop that serves limp sandwiches with fries and a lonely pickle on the side. This was a five-star restaurant, unaccustomed to whipping up lunch on demand for a frantic guest.

When I called back ten minutes later, the dinosaur within me was gaining the upper hand. "Is it done? Is it done? Is it done?" My assistant Jennifer and I had ordered a simple meal of lamb chops with vegetables and all the trimmings. I couldn't imagine what was holding them up. "Could you meet me in the lobby with the kill . . . I mean . . . the meal?" I politely inquired.

Bless the heart of our elegant continental waiter, who obviously dealt on a regular basis with pageant queens on the ragged edge of flameout. He saw no need to water down the five-star treatment just because we were going to be eating in the backseat of a speeding car. He appeared carrying a tray that held two fine china platters with silver covers, bottles of Perrier, stem goblets—the works.

A Cadillac cruised into the drive to pick us up. We took our seats in the back, the waiter placed the tray gingerly across our laps, and off we sped. The lamb chops were done to perfection, the vegetables were ideal, and the dessert looked like something out of *Bon Appetit*. It was only after a (very) quick grace that we started to dig in and realized we didn't have anything to dig in with. No silverware—not even toothpicks or straws to use as substitutes—and no napkins.

At that point, dinosaurs facing certain extinction like we were couldn't have cared less about eating utensils. I started eating the lamb chops off the bone and scooping up mashed potatoes with my fingers cave-woman style.

When I came up for air, I realized Jennifer and I were both sloshing lamb juice all over the back of our host's new Cadillac. When I began to apologize, I discovered that sticky carpet was the least of his concerns. He was a vegetarian, and his shock at seeing us carnivores devouring meat with our hands was real and profound.

It also distracted him enough to cause him to turn the wrong way up a one-way street in downtown Washington. In the spin of a steering wheel, we found ourselves headed upstream against a flood of taxis, buses, official-looking limousines, cars, trucks, motorcycles, and other assorted vehicles. After half a block or so, our host sufficiently recovered his composure to make the kind of U-turn usually seen during the last five minutes of an action-adventure movie. We pulled into the radio station parking lot, laid our tray aside, sprinted through the door, and made it to our interview right on time.

Our poor host's trials, however, were not quite over. As he was setting up a book display after the interview, he tripped over my purse, fell flat on his face, and smashed the display. I felt so responsible for his troubles, but at the same time I felt helpless. How could I have known he was a vegetarian? Was it my fault he made a klutzy move and tripped?

We always need to be sensitive to people around us whose needs and expectations are different from our own. The apostle Paul had it right in 1 Corinthians 9:22 when he said we should be "all things to all people that we may win them to Christ"—especially if they're our hosts. I was too focused on my own hunger and my interview to recognize his concerns, and he had to pay the price for my selfish oversight.

There are no words that can make up for what someone has to suffer because of our actions. All we can do is ask for God's guidance and the person's forgiveness.

The Words
of My Mouth

I'm always on the lookout for the latest trends in healthy living. When I read that I would be a healthier, happier person if all the mercury were removed from my mouth, I called my dentist immediately. "This is an emergency," I told him. "I want you to drill all the mercury fillings out of my teeth and replace them with something else, pronto."

His cordial reply could not quite hide the fact that he thought I was out of my mind.

"Don't try to talk me out of this," I said. "I'm going to have a mercury-free mouth, and I'm going to have it before my next speaking engagement." He worked me in as an emergency case, and drilled and replaced all the mercury in a single visit.

My travel partner Kay and I flew to southern California a couple of days later in preparation for an 11 A.M. Sunday service. I woke up in my hotel about two in the morning, certain that someone had taken a buzzsaw to the left side of my face. I called a local dentist, and we met in his office a little later. He told me that all the drilling had irritated three root canals, and then he spent the next several hours irritating them further.

When he finished, he said I could expect some "moderate discomfort" after the Novocain wore off, and gave me a painkiller called Vicadin.

"Doctor," I said, "I'm so sensitive to medication that I cut Advil into quarters. I've got to speak before an entire church full of people in less than twelve hours. There is no way I will be taking knock-out pills like these."

I kept my resolve for a while, but soon the pain was too intense. Audience or not, testimony or not, I had to get some relief. I took a Vicadin and finally got to sleep.

"Sleep" actually fails to describe the state I assumed. By the time I woke up, the southern California designation as La-La Land had taken on a whole new meaning. My first sensation was of Kay slapping me on the cheek.

I had overslept an hour, and was so woozy I couldn't stand up. "Wake up! Wake up!" she said over and over, like she thought I didn't hear her. I could hear perfectly—I just didn't care what she said.

"The church service is in half an hour! You've got to get up."

"OK, OK," I said (I think that's what I said). Obviously there was no way I could address a prominent California congregation if I couldn't even stand up. I called the pastor of the church and explained that I had had three root canals worked on during the night, had taken Vicadin, and was in no shape to deliver God's message.

He reminded me that we had scheduled this speaking engagement a year in advance, and that the congregation and others in the community were eagerly awaiting the story of how Mrs. United States was transformed by God from a fat, pot-smoking teenager to a fulfilled wife, mother, and inspirational speaker. He insisted my indisposition made no difference. "It is not you that speaks," he reminded me, "it is God that speaks through you."

"I know that," I drawled. "I say that too. But I'm drugged. My brain has turned to guacamole. My bottom lip is bouncing on my banner, and my heels are standing in a pool of drool."

He showed no signs of coming around to my point of view. "I'm sending someone to pick you up. They'll get you some coffee on the way."

"I don't drink caffeine."

"Today you do."

So we drove through McDonald's, got a large coffee, and my chauffeur insisted I guzzle all of it. When we got to the church, someone opened the door for me. I wanted to get out of the car, but my legs just sat there. I eventually sort of rolled over, fell out of the car, and slithered into the church. The left side of my mouth was a swollen blob from which drool hung in a very un-Mrs. United States fashion. My drug-inspired makeup job was decidedly clownlike. The pastor met me at the door, cheerfully observing, "See, I told you; there *will* be a message today." Easy for him to say.

It was about forty degrees outside, unusually cold for southern California, but I could use the weather to help me through the crisis of the moment. I warned the pastor that unless they kept the heat off and the church cold inside, I would fall asleep before I had a chance to speak; they would never be able to wake me up.

Everybody in the congregation kept their coats on, shivering. Several members asked the ushers what was wrong with the heat. One of them, unaware of the situation, headed toward the thermostat. "No!" the pastor commanded in his best fire-and-brimstone voice. "We will keep it cool, and we will have a great message delivered today."

But still, I could not stay awake. As the praise music went on, I keeled over sideways and started to snore.

The pastor dispatched two ushers to take me outside and run me around the church. Consequently, God's messenger, Mrs. United States, mouth swollen like a basketball, fast asleep in a pool of drool, was aroused from her slumber by ushers at each elbow who escort her outdoors, past a thousand people freezing their tushes off, for a high-heeled run around the church.

When they hauled me back inside, I was almost awake. I told the pastor, "If you are seriously going to make me go through with this, I need a stool." Someone set up a stool, but as the pastor introduced me, I dragged my body up to have a seat and knocked it over. I tried to bend over and pick it up, but I was afraid if I bent down that far I'd never get up again. Two ushers ran forward, picked up the stool, and sat me down on it.

The spectacle of a national beauty pageant winner swaying and drooling in front of them made even the coldest audience members forget their frozen appendages. I gazed back glassy-eyed at the stares aimed in my direction and began, "You'll have to excuse me this morning. This is *definitely* going to be God speaking and not me because I am on drugs—not drugs like I used to take, but prescription painkillers, which also seem to have killed every other sensation. I had half of my face drilled off in the middle of the night, and if I felt anything right now, I'm sure it wouldn't be good."

I spoke for fifteen minutes—and have absolutely no

idea what I said. All I remember is that as I was leaving the building, a precious fifteen-year-old girl walked up to me and told me, "You have no idea how much my life was changed today." All I could say was, "Trust me, sweetheart; it wasn't me. It was truly a touch from God."

He is strong in our weaknesses. No matter what obstacles are visible to our faltering human eyes, God will get His work done.

Not by might, nor by power,
but by my Spirit, says the Lord.
Zechariah 4:6

Excuse Me, Is Your Daughter in Trouble?

I am not normally one of those people who say, "God spoke to me and told me to tell you something." But one time I had an experience I can't explain any other way. I was seated between two large businessmen on a jam-packed airplane. I pulled out my handy-dandy inflatable neck pillow and scrunched down for a little nap, but I couldn't sleep. I thought I heard the Lord say in my spirit, "The man next to you has a daughter who is in trouble. Talk to him."

I tried to remember if I'd eaten anything recently that hadn't been properly refrigerated. *I am making things up,* I told myself. *No way. God doesn't speak to me in this way. I'm pooped, and I'm going to sleep right now.*

Every time I closed my eyes, I kept getting the same message. "The man next to you has a daughter who is in trouble. Talk to him." The man was sophisticated and elegantly dressed. He had his glasses on, reading *The Wall Street Journal.*

I said to myself, *There is no way I'm going to interrupt this guy while he is reading his paper and say, "Excuse me, is your daughter in trouble?"* I kept trying to fall asleep. It was impossible.

Okay, I reasoned silently, *if this is really God nudging me, I am going to take a chance on totally humiliating myself and ask this perfect stranger about his daughter.*

I turned to the man and said, "Excuse me, is your daughter in trouble?" For an instant his face had a shocked look as if somebody has just doused him with ice water. Then he put his head back, closed his eyes, and started to sob. He let the paper fall into his lap and took off his reading glasses. His shoulders shook and the tears ran down his face.

As soon as he could speak, he turned to me and said, "How could you possibly know that? I have a daughter who is away at college, and she is in terrible trouble. She was a virgin, and she was raped by one of her employers. Now she's pregnant." No wonder God wouldn't let me take a nap.

"The best thing I know to do, sir," I said, "is to pray. I don't know what I can say to lighten your burden. But I know that when I don't have the words, God does."

He said, "Let's pray."

We prayed for his daughter and his family. We prayed for the employer. We prayed for the baby. When we got off the plane, he called his wife immediately and said, "We need to commit our lives to God! We need to start praying for our daughter, and we need to go back to church!"

Six months later I was speaking in southern California and, to my delight, this same man came to see me. He came up to me and said, "You have no idea how your prayers changed my daughter's life. She kept the baby— she's going to put it up for adoption—and she's going to church. My wife and I have recommitted our lives to God, and we're back at church too."

My airplane conversation was a divine appointment, but I almost slept through it.

Thank You, Lord, for being persistent, for making me bold enough to risk ridicule to share Your message. All I wanted was a nap, but You had a job for me that brought Your healing hand to an entire family. Help me, like Paul, to ask for boldness, and never think I'm too busy, too tired, or too timid to do Your will.

I Wanna Quit

Even before I won the Mrs. United States title, I was heading somewhere on an airplane almost every weekend to share my testimony. Sometimes, traveling like that is tough, especially on those days when I'm already exhausted at the *beginning* of the trip. But since I won my title, I feel like I have to do more than share God's Word; I feel like people always expect me to look and act like a beauty queen. What if I'm bloated that day? What if I have PMS and ate a pound of ice cream or an entire pizza the night before? And there's always my faithful "I wanna quit" day that comes up at regular intervals, usually when I'm packing or preparing my message. But there's comfort in knowing I'm not alone.

I know everybody goes through a time in life— maybe many times—when we want to quit whatever we're doing and do something easier. When a marriage gets tough, it's tempting to toss in the towel. When a child gets rebellious, we feel like resigning from parenthood. When life gets hard, we may even feel like we want to quit life. It's the hard times, though, that make us strong. Sometimes God's greatest lessons can be learned while we're going through the fires in life. For a lot of us (me included), it's often the only way He can get our undivided attention.

One particular time when I was feeling overwhelmed by my circumstances, I decided life had simply gotten too hard to get on one more airplane and go prove that I was more than Barbie with a Bible. That was the week I heard a story that changed my life and the way that I look at ministry.

There once was a missionary who spent all of his life in a foreign land sharing the gospel and serving the Lord. He lived in a little shabby house, never had any money, and sometimes thought the whole world had forgotten about him. When he retired and sailed back to America, he happened to be traveling on the same ship as the president of the United States, who was returning home from a vacation. When the ship docked in New York, there were thousands of people and dozens of reporters and photographers there to meet and greet the president, but no one was there to greet the missionary.

The missionary found himself thinking back on a long career of selfless sacrifice and how little he had to show for his years of service. He said, "Lord, I've spent my entire life serving You. I've denied myself every worldly desire I've ever had, and yet there is no one here to welcome me home."

Then he heard the Lord say to him in his spirit, "Son, you're not home yet."

There's no party any man can throw that will match the celebration of the angels in heaven when we see our Savior face to face, and He looks at us and says, "Well done, good and faithful servant . . . enter into the joy of your Master" (Matt. 25:14, 30).

If you're a tired soldier of the Lord, you're fighting your own battle, not His. God will always give you the strength you need to serve Him. I was insisting on a rest I hadn't earned. From now on, I won't be so quick to put down my burden and put up my feet. God will tell me when it's time to celebrate.

Rescue
the Perishing

Though I've never liked to fly, I've discovered airplanes are a great place for learning about other people's faith and sharing my own. There we are, jammed in a row shoulder to shoulder with a stranger or two. We can't get away, so we may as well learn something about each other. Plus we never know when God is going to use the situation to present an unforgettable lesson.

One day I struck up a conversation with a man sitting next to me. After a few minutes, it was clear that he was a very rich, very successful businessman. After we'd been in the air for about an hour, the pilot came over the loudspeaker and said, "Ladies and gentlemen, one of our passengers has had a heart attack. We're going to have to make an emergency landing as soon as possible to get him to the hospital."

My first reaction was to close my eyes and pray silently for God to heal this person and comfort his family. Abruptly, my thoughts were interrupted by my seatmate. "I can't believe this!" he complained. "This is the third flight in a row I've been on where someone has dropped dead. Last time, a lady died right next to me, and the flight was so full they couldn't even drag her body out in the aisle. I had to sit next to it all the way to Florida!"

I couldn't decide whether to pray for this man, too, or punch him in the nose. I thought, *How could anybody be so cruel and uncompassionate?* But his remark got me thinking about us Christians and our reaction to the spiritual death all around us. Every day we sit next to someone who is dying a spiritual death, yet we think it's too embarrassing or inconvenient to stop for a moment, interrupt our day, and give him or her God's message of hope that will save their eternal lives.

Other than praying, there was nothing I could do to help the passenger who had a heart attack that day. But, like every other Christian, we have the cure for a parched and perishing spirit. God, grant us the courage to share it.

Coupon Truckin'

My father is one of the most impatient men I have ever known. One particular example of his time-saving technique has taken its place of honor in the family lore.

When I was a young girl, I was standing in line at the grocery store with my father. We had only three or four items and went to a line where there was just one woman in front of us, who looked like she was about to finish checking out. When the checker rang up her total, she hauled out a gigantic wad of coupons from her purse. I don't know how many there were, but from my perspective it looked like somewhere in the low thousands.

She fiddled with the coupons, occasionally handing one to the checker who matched it with the item purchased. Dad, never one to simmer for long when he could enjoy the pleasure of blowing up, bounced on the balls of his feet for a minute, then stepped up to the lady.

The lady and the checker interrupted their transaction to look at my father. "How much are her groceries?" Dad demanded. The checker told him. "I'll pay for her groceries! Give me those —— coupons and get out of my way!" Dad then snatched the coupons and maniacally shredded them into confetti, which showered onto the conveyor and down the way to an astonished bag boy.

I'll never forget the expression on that poor woman's face—a combination of surprise, disgust, astonishment, and thanks that I've never seen before or since. If you're on a tight budget, you might want to get in the grocery line in front of my dad and then move *reeeally* slowly.

At the time, I thought my father was funny and cool. If the same thing were to happen today, I hope I'd recognize it as a divine appointment. My steps, even in the checkout line, are ordered of the Lord. Maybe I'm supposed to pray for a stranger or give a word of encouragement to a flustered cashier. Or even offer an understanding smile and calming touch to an impatient, irrepressible man I love very much.

Fighting Time

I tend to assume that if I'm really busy, I must be doing something productive. Dad always used to say, "Sheri, I'm fighting time! Get out of my way; I'm fighting time!" Now I understand what he was talking about. And I've also learned that if you fight time on time's terms, you will *always* lose.

If the devil can't make us bad, his next trick is to make us busy. If he can keep us busy doing things that are insignificant and without eternal value, he can keep us from our divine appointments, and he can keep us from hearing God's Word clearly when God is speaking to us. He can steal our joy.

There is nothing worse than not knowing where we're going, and killing ourselves to get there. Some days Steve will come home and say, "What did you do today?" "I was so busy!" I'll reply exhaustedly. Then he'll say, "Well, what'd you do?" I have no idea. But I was so busy doing it!

It reminds me of the advice the Cheshire cat gave to Alice in Wonderland when she asked him which path to take at an intersection.

"Where are you going?" the cat asked.

"I have no idea," replied Alice.

"When you don't know where you're going, any road will do," the cat observed.

I've finally realized that if something has no significant and eternal value, it doesn't deserve my time. This is not a dress rehearsal. I'll never get this day again. "Sheri, don't waste time fighting time," I remind myself. "Use it to do something that brings glory to God." I don't always succeed, of course, but the days I do is time well spent.

Make the most of your time,
for the days are evil.
Ephesians 5:16

Warriors, Not Worriers

I am a fanatic about praying for angels to protect everybody. I pray for my car. I pray over airplanes when I fly. I pray for my little boy every day that God will station angels around him. I pray over my friends.

One particular day, however, I had forgotten to pray. I was riding in a car with a lady who was telling me about a young mother who had just been killed in a freak accident. Her young friend, with two babies in the backseat, was following a big truck on a California highway. The

129

truck swerved unexpectedly, and a tire bounced out of the back, sailed through the air, smashed the car's windshield, and killed the mother instantly.

Not surprisingly, that was the exact moment when I realized I had not prayed yet for our trip. So I interrupted the lady and said, "Do you mind if I pray?" Though I always ask, I've never had anybody say, "Nah, I don't think you need to do that. Let's just skip it." She said, "Of course I don't mind. I'd be pleased if you did."

I started to pray, "God, please protect this car. Put angels all about it. Let your blood cover our car." I kept on and kept on, and I knew the lady was beginning to think I was a freak or something because I was so determined to start praying at that exact moment; and for some reason, I felt like I wanted to keep on praying.

Seconds after I finished, we were cruising down the freeway when a big truck in front of us swerved unexpectedly. A tire stored in the back of it flew out and headed directly toward our windshield at sixty miles an hour. Now it was the lady's turn to freak-out. She was screaming, "Oh Jesus, please help us! Please help us!" at the absolute top of her lungs. She was shaking so hard she lost control of the car. The woman, my assistant Tanna, and I all saw the tire coming directly toward us. Then we all saw it physically moved to the side just before it would have crashed through our windshield.

No one who witnessed it could doubt that God

moved that tire out of our path. No law of physics in the natural world could have done it. Without God and His angels, the three of us would have been "tire burgers" on the Santa Monica Freeway.

God can be trusted to listen to our prayers and respond to them. He has called us to be prayer warriors, not prayer worriers. The lesson I learned on the freeway that day was that whenever God puts someone or something on your heart, don't wait to pray about it. A warrior has to be ready at a moment's notice. Your prayer in the car, on the phone, at the office, or in the checkout line could be the interceding force that changes someone's life and eternal destiny.

A warrior must also have a source for his power. No matter how skilled a soldier he might be, he would never walk into a battle alone or unarmed. He always seeks the power and wisdom of his commanding officer. That power doesn't come from crystals or people, or even dead saints. God, through His Son, Jesus Christ, is the only power capable of saving you. It's great to know He wants to be that source. Once you feel God's power as a prayer warrior, you never have to be a worrier again.

Patience
in God's Garden

When I first became a Christian, I all but tripped strangers on the street to tell them about the Lord. I witnessed to grocery store clerks, dry cleaners—anyone standing within shouting distance would hear about the wonderful saving relationship that I had with Jesus Christ. I was a fanatic! I embarrassed more mature Christians. Twenty-four hours a day I ate, slept, and breathed the Word of God. I wanted the whole world to know that they could be set free.

I could tell anybody about the Lord—except my own Jewish family.

It took me six months to tell my father what had happened. He was sitting across the table from me at dinner one night, and he said, "You seem so different somehow. I've never seen you with such joy and such peace. I've never seen you so content just being where you are."

I told Dad that six months ago I had been a hopeless, suicidal wreck. But Jesus—the Jesus he had told me was not the Messiah—had come into my heart and changed my life, healed me from my broken past, and had become my Savior.

I had never been more afraid to tell my father anything. I had no idea how he would react. Would he scream at me? Order me out of the house forever? Nothing could have prepared me for what happened next.

Tears filled my father's eyes. He looked at me for a long minute, then said, "Whatever it took, I'm so glad you have it because I love you very much. Just don't tell our family, and especially don't tell your grandmother about your new faith in Christ." (Dad always liked peace at all costs.)

When I was a child, my Jewish grandmother was the only woman in my life who had ever told me she loved me. She was my best friend when I was a little girl, the one I went to for comfort and love. Soon after that dinner with Dad, I found out that my grandmother was dying. I wanted her to spend eternity with me, so I gathered up all the courage I could and went to her house to visit her.

I'd been to her home many times before, but this time I hesitated. The lights were on and the windows were wide open, but somehow, it felt very dark as I entered her room. We looked at each other for a moment and smiled awkwardly. Then, feeling a sudden sense of urgency, I crawled up into the bed, laid my body over hers, and said, "Grandma, I want you to go to heaven with me."

"I will sweetheart," she answered weakly.

"Grandma," I said, "you need Jesus as your Savior so you can go to heaven with me."

Mustering all the strength she could, she turned her back to me and faced the wall. "Get out of my house," she snapped bitterly. "You're the one who's dead. Don't come to my funeral. I never want to see you again."

My father was furious that I had told Grandma about my new life as a Christian after he'd ordered me not to. No one in the family would talk to me. I was not invited to my grandmother's funeral. My father stayed mad for over a year, and during that time there were many nights when I wondered if I had done the right thing. Under the circumstances, should I have been obedient to God's Word? Or should I have kept my mouth shut in order to keep the peace?

That year was one of the loneliest, darkest years of my life. But the seed of faith that God planted in my dad at dinner eventually grew. In time, he came to accept Christ. Today, my whole family is born again in the Lord. I was patient because I didn't have a choice. But God honored my patience anyway, with a harvest greater than anything I could ever have imagined.

Even These Hairs Are Numbered

I come from a long line of hair-obsessed people, and I feel secure in saying I will be continuing the tradition.

I have some indelible memories of my father standing in front of the mirror with his special brush and blow dryer and a can of hair spray. He had (and still has) basically four tufts of hair which he individually sculpted for an hour at a time. If he could not get his four patches of hair to lie down straight, he would not leave the house. I remember him canceling business meetings at the office because his hair would not cooperate.

On bad hair days he would scream and yell and run around the house. On good hair days he enjoyed having an audience as he arranged the *coiffure du jour,* and would sometimes make us kids get out of bed, sit in the bathroom, and watch him blow-dry his hair.

Growing up with such an example, I was a sucker for every shampoo, conditioner, treatment, and hair gimmick on TV. Several years ago I saw a commercial for clip-on hair extensions. What a great concept! You take these pieces of fake hair and clip them into your own hair for a fuller, thicker look in minutes. If Farrah Fawcett could do it, couldn't I?

I had a big Christmas presentation to make in Arkansas, so I bought a pair of these clip-on hair pieces to get the thick, luxurious hair I had always dreamed about in time for the trip. Not one to be burdened by un-necessary instructions, I put them on having no idea how they worked. I spoke on Friday night and everything went great, my new lush locks framing my face just so.

As I went to the podium for the final conference session on Saturday night, the lady who introduced me gave me a big old bear hug. *These people are so sweet,* I thought. I continued walking toward the microphone unaware that her embrace had unclipped one of my spiffy new hair extensions. Beginning my remarks, I couldn't help noticing that my audience seemed preoccupied. Tanna, my manager, kept pointing to her ear. I thought she needed a Q-tip or something.

It wasn't until I finished and sat down that I saw half of my lush locks cascading down the back of my jacket and sticking out under my armpit. I looked like I was carrying a ferret. It was a testament to the power of God's message that I didn't get laughed off the stage. But despite the distraction, we actually felt a tremendous sense of outreach that weekend and saw many people give their lives to Christ.

The hair obsession that had so absorbed both my father and me really served no purpose that weekend in Arkansas, or any other time in my life. If you think about it, there are probably things in your own life that really don't matter, yet they have become or are becoming an obsession. They drain your energy from more productive tasks and distract you from doing God's work. I challenge you today to search yourself and ask if there's an obsession in your life greater than serving and loving the Lord. Let us run the race unencumbered.

The Massage Is Clear

I needed a vacation. Boy, did I need a vacation! I had been traveling, Steve had been busy with his graphic design business, and we were both frazzled. Finally the week we had so carefully carved out was just around the corner, and I began to make preparations for our escape.

It was quickly apparent that we wouldn't get far. We had exactly one hundred dollars in the piggy bank, and seventy of those were spoken for as a tithe we owed from the week before. The thought crossed my mind that we could "borrow" the seventy dollars until another check came in, and no one ever had to know. But then again, God keeps His promises to us, and it didn't seem right for us not to keep our promise to tithe. So we gave Him the seventy bucks and prepared for an exotic vacation filled with wonderful adventures—like weeding flower beds and waxing cars.

Well, it's a good thing God doesn't take vacations, and, as usual, we were reminded that you can never out-give God. A few days later we received a check for five hundred dollars along with a note that said, "We want you to have this for your vacation so you can enjoy your time off and be refreshed by the Lord."

I had great plans for that five hundred dollars! The first order of business was to schedule a massage. I hadn't had one in ages, and my shoulder blades were creeping closer to my earlobes every day. I was on my way to looking like a bowling pin, and this financial blessing rescued me just in time.

I called the beauty salon (where all vacations should begin) to get my nails done, then made an appointment with the massage therapist. She only had one opening left all week, at three o'clock that afternoon. I finished at the manicurist and got in the car to drive over to my soothing, relaxing, invigorating, luxurious massage. I turned the key and nothing happened. No sputtering and dying, no rrr . . . rrr . . . rrr. Zero.

I could not believe it! The car was almost new, and it was one of those utility vehicles that was supposed to go anywhere. All I wanted was to go five miles down a level concrete highway to a massage therapist whose only remaining appointment before our vacation was all mine unless I missed it, in which case my shoulder blades would fuse permanently together.

Just then a man walked by and said, "Can I help you with your car?" He opened the hood and started to poke and jiggle various wires, hoses, and other automotive gizmos. "What do you do?" he asked. I was not in the mood for conversation. All I could think about was getting to my massage. I said, "I'm an evangelist."

He raised up with an astonished look on his face and said, "Man, I can't believe this! All people can talk to me about all of a sudden is God! When I'm at work, people talk to me about God. When I'm at the gym, people talk to me about God. Even my girlfriend has been talking to me about God!"

Not now Lord! No divine appointment this afternoon! I thought. *Have You forgotten I'm about to miss my massage? If I do, your servant will be worthless because everybody will think she's a penguin disguised as Mrs. United States.*

The more I thought about it, though, the more I realized what was going on. After a five-second prayer that I'd say the right thing, I told the man, "OK, the reason my car won't start, and the reason people keep talking to you about God is because He is calling you into a relationship with Him. This is a divine appointment. Now could you hurry and fix my car so I can get to my massage?"

At that moment I felt a special kinship with Jonah. (You know, the guy in the Bible who God allowed to be inconvenienced until he got his attention.) The instant after I shared that little message, my car started immediately. The man had no idea why. I had a theory of my own, but it had nothing to do with alternators. I gave the guy one of my tapes and said, "Please listen to this. God has prepared your heart for this moment, and now this tape will tell you about something you weren't ready to hear until now."

He thanked me with a smile, and I hopped into the car, praising God for such a wonderful opportunity. I even made it to my massage on time. After all, to shoulder the responsibility of witnessing at my next opportunity, I have to have shoulders.

A Picture
of Forgiveness

During my reign as Mrs. United States, *Women First* magazine came to our house and took pictures of Steve, Jacob, and me doing things around the house—roller-blading, cooking, tucking Jacob in at night, and other day-in-the-life-of situations.

One shot they wanted was of me in an evening gown at sunset on the red rocks at Squaw Peak near our house in Phoenix—not exactly day-in-the-life stuff. Picture, if you will, my family and a herd of photographers, editors, and assorted other magazine types hiking over rocks, cactus, shrubs, and a variety of desert critters on our way to the top.

While everyone else was dressed in appropriately rugged clothing, I was in full pageant regalia: evening gown, major high heels, my "Mrs. United States 1994" banner whipping in the wind, and my crown teetering atop my windblown hairdo. In the first pageant I ever won, I fell off the stage in a flat, wind-free auditorium. Here I was forging my own wilderness path up the side of a desert mountain—in sequins. "It'll be the greatest shot in the article," they promised. Fine.

Normally, when my family and I go places we pray over our car and our belongings and entrust them to God. But this particular photo shoot, Steve and I were so consumed with my having to get up to the top of this hill in an evening gown that we had forgotten to pray. When we finished the photo shoot and skidded back down the hill, we found that someone had broken into our car.

Steve's wallet and a few other valuables were missing, but that was small potatoes compared to the real crime. Some terrible person had stolen my face! All my makeup was gone—three hundred dollars worth!

I would much rather have had him steal the car! That, I could have replaced. But when I carefully, scientifically, and lovingly put my makeup kit together, when I get my lipstick in just the right shape so that it fits my

146

lips, well, . . . I mean, this was a tragedy. Mrs. United States without her face!

As I sat there stunned, wondering whether the robber and I had compatible skin tones, my little boy said, "Why don't we pray for the thief?" Sometimes God's message comes in the cutest packages.

"That's an excellent idea," I said. "We can pray that God will restore all of our belongings and let us meet this thief and let him know that we forgive him and so does God." The photographer looked at me skeptically. "Oh yeah, I'm sure the thief is going to be sitting there by himself and have a change of heart. He'll knock on your door and say, 'Here I am to deliver all of your belongings that I swiped.'"

Before you could say, "OK, cowboy, drop that mascara!" the Shepherd family circled the "wagons," joined hands, and started to pray—not only for our belongings to be returned, but that we would be able to meet or somehow minister to the person who had stolen them. As the photographer watched and listened, I hoped we would be a good "picture" for him of what our God could do.

A little later, Steve's cellular phone rang. It was a police officer who said they had recovered stolen property that evidently belonged to us; they had the thief in custody, and wanted us to identify our belongings. The officer asked if we wanted to press charges. We told him no, but that we would like to come down to the police station and meet the man.

Walking into the police station, the first thing I saw was my makeup kit (so real forgiveness and healing *was* possible). Steve's wallet and our other things were there as well. The officers didn't let us meet the man, but they let us write him a letter and send him a ministry tape. In the letter we wrote, "We just want you to know that we forgive you and that we don't want to press charges. God forgives you, too, and He loves you."

If you're ever the unfortunate victim of a robbery or break-in, you'll be shocked and disappointed. That's human nature. But you'll also find yourself with a rare and wonderful opportunity to reflect on what it meant when God paid the price for our sins, sacrificing Himself so that we, the criminals, could go free.

Security
Blanket

Whenever I hear a scary story, I become convinced that the same terrifying thing will happen to me at any minute. (Is that the wind blowing, or is someone about to leap out of the bushes and conk me on the head?) Common sense would suggest that I avoid listening to scary stories, but common sense does not always have the upper hand in life.

Not long ago, a friend told me about a gas station attendant who had come over to a customer's car window.

The customer asked for a fill-up. The attendant filled her tank and went back to the window to get her credit card. Glancing in the backseat, he noticed a gunman hiding on the floor. The attendant went inside for a minute, then came back out and said, "Ma'am, your credit card isn't working, and you'll have to come into the office."

Naturally the woman was in a hurry. "Here, let me give you another card," she said.

"No, ma'am" he replied. "It's very important that you get out of the car and take this phone call from the credit card company. They absolutely insist on talking to you."

The young attendant had called the police, and as the woman picked up the phone, the police arrived and arrested the gunman. That young man probably saved her life.

After hearing this story, I had a severe case of the creeps and spent the rest of the afternoon checking the backseat of my car as I drove around. My mother-in-law's van was on the street in front of our house when I got home. Steve was busy in the garage and asked if I would back the van into the driveway so we could load it up.

I hopped in, started the engine, and put the gearshift in reverse. Glancing in the rearview mirror, I thought I saw the shape of a man in the backseat. I didn't see his gun, but no doubt it was just behind the seat. Stricken with terror and seeing no gas station attendant nearby, I jumped out and started sprinting across the neighbors' front yard.

After running a few steps, I turned to see if the gunman was following me. He wasn't, but the van was. I had left it in reverse, and it was backing across the grass directly toward the neighbors' living room window. I ran like a maniac and grabbed the open driver's side door, trying to use my tennis shoes as brakes.

At that moment, my husband looked up to see what all the commotion was about and saw me locked in mortal combat with a minivan headed for death and destruction. Steve came dashing out of the house, jumped in through the passenger's side, and threw on the brakes just as I was beginning to plow through the front flower bed. We missed the front window by less than a foot.

Peeking into the backseat, I saw that my armed assailant was in fact an extremely lifelike blanket. It was an unforgettable lesson in how easy it is to overreact to attacks that may never happen to me personally. I had allowed the gas station story to foster fearful and carelessness. Focusing on my fear made me forget that my Protector is always beside me.

When Jesus' disciples were caught in an awful storm in the Sea of Galilee, their fear was heart-stopping. Their fear was real. Their fear was unfounded. Jesus was with them then as He is with us now.

Enough real problems exist in the world, so there's no sense in making up problems of our own.

Icebreaker SOS

When a group of women get together for a retreat without their husbands and children, there is no telling what will happen. At one particular gathering not long ago, the planners decided to have an ice-breaking game before I began my presentation. They divided us into Group A and Group B and had a contest to see which group could turn in the most items from their collective purses.

First they called for lipsticks, and we all dug around in our purses to fish out our Cantaloupe Blush or Pouty

Persimmon, or whatever, and passed it to the front. The next category was receipts, then breath mints, and so on down the line. The sides were pretty evenly matched, and by the final round the score was tied at nine points each. Whoever won the next round would be Purse Scavenger Champs, with bragging rights for the whole weekend.

I was sitting with Group A, and Group A smelled victory right around the corner. We were pumped. The moderator prepared to announce the last category, pausing for dramatic effect as we sat with hands poised over our pocketbooks. "And now the championship category is . . . tweezers!"

One of my teammates in the back of the room pulled a pair of tweezers out of her bag and launched them toward the front instead of passing them, time being an essential element in going for the gold. The tweezers flew through the air to where I sat on the front row, and stuck like a blow dart in the back of my head. When I turned to see what had happened (was the other side attacking us?), the tweezers fell out of my scalp, bounced off my shoulder, ricocheted off my lap, and ran my hose from knee to heel.

Now, of course, it was time for me to speak. Bloodied and battle scarred (at least we won), with no time to repair the damage, I took my place at the lectern. To my left was a big speaker box. "Is this in your way?" I asked the audience. "Yes!" they all shouted. Trying to be useful, I began loosening the clamp on the speaker stand so I could lower it. Unfortunately, gravity had other plans, persuading the speaker cabinet to slide down the stand with a hair-raising screech and pinch my hand. My eyes bulged. My heart pounded. My hand throbbed.

Five hundred women gasped at the sight of their guest being attacked by a cabinet full of woofers and tweeters. I didn't think I was seriously hurt—nothing ice packs and a week of bed rest couldn't improve—and tried to make light of the whole thing. "Sometimes I break a nail right before I speak," I joked, "and I always think that means my message is going to be anointed. Since I've just punctured my head, run my hose, and broken my hand, this will probably be the best message I've ever given."

Everyone laughed, the tension was broken, and I launched into the presentation. About thirty seconds into my remarks, I had just spoken the sentence, "I don't think the devil would want me to deliver this message today." At that instant a potted plant above me tipped over on its side, sending a substantial shower of mulch, dirt, and vermiculite all over me and the lectern.

I had expected to teach by word rather than by example that day, but God had other plans. The title of my program? "How Do You React to Trial and Tribulation?"

Welcome Home,
Honey

One day I was in a restaurant for lunch with three pastors' wives. When the young waiter came up to take our order, he saw that all of us wore wedding rings. He said, "Oh no, four wives together. Another lunchtime husband-bashing."

All four of us started talking at once. "No, we love our husbands. We're not going to sit here and talk mean about them behind their backs." He said, "You've got to be kidding. You wouldn't believe what I hear around here when wives get going about what slimeballs their husbands are." We insisted that we all loved our husbands and were not meeting to plan a verbal assault.

This young man was so shocked and amazed that he could not stay away from our table. Before he left with our orders, he asked how we could be happily married when so many women seemed to do nothing but complain about their spouses. He asked more questions when he came back with our drinks and had another set ready that he served up with our salads. By the time the check came I was considering charging him a seminar fee.

But the more I considered his reaction, the more I realized I shouldn't have been surprised. As women, we tend to be a teensy little bit whiny once in a while. We can give our husbands, our children, and people around us the impression that we're no longer in love with the men we married.

Think about it. How many times have our husbands come home from dodging the slings and arrows of outrageous fortune all day, and we collapse pitifully in their arms as soon as they walk in the door, saying, "I'm exhausted; I'm bloated; the dishes aren't done; the house is a mess; the kids were rotten today; the car broke down; and, by the way, welcome home, honey. I love you"?

His natural reaction is to make a beeline for the recliner and the TV remote, searching frantically for the "wife mute" button. We would never have greeted them that way when we were first married. Not that we shouldn't share the trials and frustrations of the day, but the bad stuff didn't use to be the first and most intensely felt things out of our mouths. Many times we do not treat our husbands to the warm welcome we once did, and their reaction shows it. But if we treat someone—anyone—preciously, they will become precious to us.

Occasionally during the day, we'll find ourselves treating a perfect stranger better than we treat our own husbands. That's backward from the way God intended things to be. We should be more conscious of the way we treat our spouses than of the way we treat anyone else, because they are our precious gift from God. (And also because, unlike a stranger, we have to face them again the next day!)

In speech, conduct, love, faith and purity,
show yourself an example of those who believe.
1 Timothy 4:12, NASB

Our Gang

Steve and I were in Seattle producing a showcase for models, actors, and singers. We had auditioned more than 1,300 people and had just met for our first rehearsal with the 150 talented individuals who had been selected to participate in the production.

While the applicants who had made the cut were still preparing for rehearsal to begin, I noticed a grubby gang of rowdy teenagers in the lobby who were about to be booted out onto the street by the security guard. *These ruf-*

fians couldn't possibly be part of our show, I thought to my-self as I approached cautiously to confirm my assumption.

No sooner had I said that when two of the boys rec-ognized me. I gulped. Obviously, they were two of the thousand-plus who had auditioned for our showcase and didn't have what it takes. What are they doing here? What are they *wearing?* Their outfits made Seattle grunge look like high fashion. This was all I needed—gang members causing problems for our crew and all our young performers!

Feeling like a protective mamma bear, I watched as the security guard escorted them out, pointed a finger at them, then turned and walked back inside. I mumbled a prayer of thanks as I headed back to the rehearsal.

While I was praying, God grabbed my attention with the verse, "Man looks at the outward appearance, but God looks at the heart." My first thought was that no-body would ever make it in Hollywood following that verse. But then again, this showcase was meant first to get people to heaven, not Hollywood.

I knew what I had to do. God wanted me to invite those two gang members to spend the week working with us on our showcase. I quickly walked outside the lobby and there, as if on cue, the two boys turned and faced me. I was scared to death. I glanced around, hop-ing to find that security guard. Seeing he was nowhere to be found, I got a death grip on my clipboard, arms folded across my chest, and stepped forward cautiously thinking, *I'm either hearing from God now, or I'm going to meet Him tonight.*

"I know you both auditioned for the showcase," I stammered. They were obviously surprised that I would speak to them other than to tell them to get lost before I called the cops. "Rehearsal is starting, and you both better get in there right away."

It took a moment for my words to sink in. I was inviting them to join us for the showcase.

"Forget it, Barbie!" the leader finally sneered. "We weren't picked 'cause we don't got no talent."

"And no money," his sidekick added.

"Well I think you'll do great in this showcase," I replied, "and I should know. I'm the director. And as far as money goes, your entry fee has been taken care of. So what do you say?"

They turned to look at each other through long, scraggly hair. "Cool!" they blurted, throwing their cigarettes down and following me inside. I wasn't quite sure which category to put them in. Modeling? Acting? How about a new category for body odor?

When we got to the room, the rehearsal was just about to begin. I introduced my new counterculture buddies to the staff, and we went on with business as usual.

The two boys were back the next day. Steve and I both made a point of greeting them and making them welcome. We told them they were precious to God and that we were glad they had decided to join us. By the third day (praise God!) they'd decided to take showers. The fourth day, one of the boys couldn't wait to come in and tell me he didn't smoke any pot the night before, and the other proudly announced he'd decided to quit smoking.

At the final dress rehearsal, when I shared my testimony and my husband shared the message of salvation, these two boys were the very first to come forward and give their lives to Jesus Christ. At the end of the altar call they walked up to Steve and me and said, "Could you be our spiritual parents?"

One of the boys continued, "When we were six and seven years old, our parents pushed us out of a car while they were driving through downtown Seattle, and we've never seen them again." He explained that ever since, they had been bounced around in the foster care system from one home to another.

"Right now we're hiding out, and we're afraid."

All their lives, these boys had been told how bad they were. Even Christians they'd met before were quick to point the finger and say, "Look at all the poor choices you've made!" Now they had proof that God loved them and had a plan for their lives.

By word and deed, Christians have to let the world know that we don't have to get right *before* we can come to Jesus. Come to Jesus, and He'll make us right.

Is There Chocolate in Heaven?

As a little girl, I used to dream about being a princess. I would wear my mom's high heels, and my dad would bring me flowers. I made fake banners and pretended that I was Princess of the World.

The moment I gave my life to the Lord at the age of twenty-four, I realized that I was then a princess for real, because when I became a Christian, I became a daughter of the King. Every Christian has a reign on earth, and a job and responsibility that come with that reign. Every day we have a divine appointment, and every day our steps are ordered of the Lord.

One of the definitions of a crown is "an emblem of glory signifying a position of honor or power." The interesting thing is that a crown has no power or real significance of its own. In fact, it doesn't even sparkle while sitting in the dark. It isn't like a beauty pageant crown the winner keeps for a year and then gives away to next year's winner. It's a crown of unfading glory because it reflects the majesty and glory of God, and once it's ours, we get to keep it forever.

When the King of kings is our father, we get a prize package far greater than anything we will ever see on any game show or beauty pageant. As a son or daughter of the King, our prize package includes: no more sickness, no more tears, no more death, a crystal sea, streets of gold, a mansion built by God Himself, and an eternal crown that no one can take from us.

As I've looked at the eternal prize package, the one thing that I can't seem to find anywhere is chocolate. I've searched all through the Bible without success. Why would God have me hanging out with my girlfriends by the crystal sea and on the streets of gold and not have an unlimited supply of chocolate? So close to perfection and yet so far.

But, folks, I have it figured out. The reason there probably won't be chocolate in heaven is that there won't be stress in heaven either, so we won't need chocolate!

The next time you feel discouraged, remember that you have an incredible inheritance waiting just for you: everything you need, nothing you don't, and all of eternity to enjoy it. It's easy to get so caught up in what we don't have that we lose sight of the gifts that God gives us every day. If we all got what we deserved according to His standards, we'd end up with nothing. Praise God for His grace in making us sons and daughters of the King.

Daughter of the King

I had just finished speaking in New York City on the royal call in 1 Peter 2:9, which says we are God's special people, a royal priesthood who "may proclaim the excellencies of Him who has called you out of darkness into His marvelous light" (NASB).

"If we pray for a divine appointment to share the gospel every day," I said confidently, "God will give us one."

The pastor of the church where I spoke, along with his wife, spent the next day sightseeing with Steve and me. Before we started out, the pastor suggested, "Let's pray for one of those divine appointments you've been talking about."

What a great idea, I thought. *This is the Big Apple. There certainly couldn't be a shortage of hurting people here.*

We prayed and then set out to make the rounds of all the famous tourist attractions. We saw the Statue of Liberty, drank tea at the Plaza Hotel, ice skated at Rockefeller Center, and saw the World Trade Center. But as the sun set over the Jersey shore, not a single door had been opened for a divine appointment.

I was getting ready to trip someone so I could pick them up, apologize, and tell them about Jesus. I kept waiting and praying and looking for an opportunity to tell somebody—anybody—about the Lord. I wondered to myself if God had heard our prayer that morning. It would look really bad if I taught this message about sharing the Word of God every day and then didn't follow through.

About 10:00 P.M. we stopped in a coffee shop for a bite to eat before heading back to the pastor's house for the night. Two beautiful young girls came in after we did and sat at the next table. We were near the theater district, and one of the girls walked up to me and said, "Are you a celebrity?"

Recognizing my cue I said, "Yes. I am a daughter of the King. My Father created the heavens and the earth."

Finally my appointment had showed up. The two girls looked at each other, then back at me. "What does that mean?" the other one asked.

"You know that God created the heavens and the earth?" I asked.

"Yes," she answered.

"Well, Jesus is my Savior," I explained. "So that means I have a relationship with God, and that makes me His daughter. My God is the King of kings and Lord of lords."

We talked with the two girls all the way through their dinner. Under any other circumstances, I would have excused myself and attacked my caesar salad. But they were listening so intently, I forgot all about it.

"Well," one of the girls said after half an hour, "I could never accept this Jesus and become a daughter of the King because I'm Jewish."

"What a coincidence!" I exclaimed. "So is my Savior. And so am I." I shared my testimony with the girls, and Steve shared Scriptures with them about God's eternal plan for their lives. As I was going over all that God had done in my life—how He had delivered me out of drug abuse, bulimia, a broken heart, and a broken home—one of the girls started to cry.

"I just got out of a drug rehab program last week," she said. "Say, are you guys angels?"

"No," I answered, "but we are messengers, and this is the divine appointment we prayed for this morning. You see, God arranged for us to meet you here today so that we could give you a message of hope and eternal life. And now we would love to invite you to become daughters of the King yourselves and receive the eternal crown, so that you can experience God's peace in your life today and enjoy His presence for all eternity."

Right there in the restaurant, those two girls accepted Jesus as their savior and became daughters of the King. What a wonderful, glorious day it was! How different the story would have been if all Steve and I had had to talk about was how rude New Yorkers are, how expensive the food is, and how much our feet hurt. Every day, our steps are ordered of the Lord, and our conversation can cause people to thirst for righteousness in Christ.

As Mrs. United States I won a crown and banner. But infinitely more important, I have a crown that is eternal, a banner that is God's love, and the privilege of wearing the name of Jesus on my heart always. Never stop looking for the divine appointment He has waiting for you every day of the year, every year of your life.

Rachel

I f you know the Lord Jesus as your Savior, you are a child of the King. Each one of God's children has a royal call on their lives (1 Pet. 2:9). I had the privilege of knowing a beautiful young girl who took her reign on earth seriously. She was a true princess who kept divine appointments every day of her life. Her name was Rachel. She went to a public school that was more like a war zone than a place to learn. Drugs were everywhere. Gangs terrorized the students. Godly values were nonexistent.

During her freshman year, when she was thirteen, Rachel began to feel tired all the time and lost her appetite. A trip to the doctor brought tragic news: Rachel had leukemia.

The diagnosis left Rachel with a choice: become bitter or better. Rachel had no room for bitterness in her life. "I don't know how long I have to live," she told her parents, "and I know that God can choose to heal me. But I'm going to bring as many people home with me into eternity as I can. I'm committed to making every day count for Jesus." Rachel asked her parents to hold her accountable and pray over her every day before school that God would give her a divine appointment with a schoolmate.

The rumor had spread through her school that she had cancer, so all eyes were on her every day. This trial gave Rachel a chance to show her classmates the peace and joy only God can bring in such a tragic situation. In a way, she was blessed in her affliction because she could grasp more intently the truth that our days are numbered. In the Bible, Peter reminds us that we are strangers and aliens in this place. We are only visitors.

The kids at school could not understand why, even though she was dying, Rachel was so concerned about them. She shared the love of Christ with everyone she could. On her sixteenth birthday, she told her parents, "I'm ready to go home and be with the Lord now. I just want to bring my high school with me." That night, she wrote a letter to her school. A few weeks later, Rachel answered God's call to be with Him in heaven.

Rachel's mother asked the principal if her daughter's classmates could come to the funeral to hear the letter Rachel wrote. It was only when the principal announced Rachel's funeral that the full impact of her three years of evangelism became clear. Hundreds of students requested permission to go, and a fleet of school buses carried them from the campus to the funeral. I was in the enormous crowd as the pastor began to read: "Dear Classmates: I told my parents that I was willing to die and go home into eternity if I could bring all of you with me. My Savior made a way for you to get to the other side. . . ."

After the letter was finished, the pastor looked up and asked, "How many of you want to see Rachel some day on the other side of eternity?" Almost every student in the room surged forward to give their lives to Jesus Christ.

How many of those kids will grow up to be godly parents? How many will become pastors, teachers, and evangelists? Because one princess understood she had a royal call on her life and kept her divine appointments, she changed people's lives for eternity.

I challenge you today: when you've gone to be with Jesus, what will you be remembered for? What do you want to be remembered for? Life is not a dress rehearsal. When it's over, it's over. Live this day as if it's your last, and watch what happens to you and everyone around you.

Life Is Not a Dress Rehearsal

E very day, each of us gets only one chance to live for Christ. The opportunities we have to witness for Him that day will never come again. We can't keep waiting for something big to happen. It's happening now, as you read this.

If the curtain comes down and this is your last day, will you go to heaven? Are you sure? God tells us there's only one way to heaven, and He made it possible for us to get there by sending His only Son to die so that we might live. (Read John 3:16–17.)

I heard a true story that gives me some sense of the sacrifice God made for me. There was a man who worked on a drawbridge, lowering it when trains were scheduled to come across, but otherwise keeping it raised so ships could pass underneath.

The father had one child, a son, whom he loved bringing to work with him. Every day they would visit together in the tiny cab high on the bridge where the controls were. They ate lunch together and watched boats go by underneath them.

One day the man heard the whistle of a train. An unscheduled express was barreling down the track, headed for the drawbridge at full speed. He ran to the controls to lower the bridge, but as he looked out the window, he saw his young son had fallen in the gear mechanism. His mind raced frantically for a solution, but he knew there wasn't time to rescue the boy and lower the bridge. This left the man with a horrible choice. He could leave the bridge up, saving his son and killing the hundreds of passengers on the train, or he could lower the bridge, crushing his son in the gears but allowing the train to cross safely.

With his trembling hands gripping the lever that would, in an instant, be both an instrument of salvation and of destruction, he looked through tear-filled eyes, casting one last look down at his only son. Then he closed his eyes, turned his head, and pulled the lever that lowered the bridge. As the train went by, he saw passengers inside talking, eating, reading newspapers, or napping, completely unaware of the sacrifice he had made so they could live.

Every day, so many of us take life for granted, never giving God a thought, never acknowledging that He allowed His Son to die so we could live eternally in heaven with Him. There was no other way to save us. The cross is no longer a symbol of death and sacrifice; it is a symbol of life everlasting. That is a sacrifice we cannot afford to waste. Every day counts. There is no rehearsal. There is only the daily reality of the cross, our salvation—and God's infinite love.

Who's running the show in your life so far? You or the One who created you?

If you were to leave this life today, what would you be remembered for? What would you wish you had done, or wish you hadn't done? Does anyone in your life today need to hear you say, "Thank you," "I love you," or "I'm sorry?"

Receive God's Greatest Gift

Every day God offers you the gift of eternal life. If you have already accepted this priceless gift, promise today to rededicate yourself to making every day a day you live for Him—not a dress rehearsal but a command performance for the King of kings.

If you have not asked God into your heart, it is my prayer that you will ask Him now to forgive your sins and be your Lord and Savior. Claim God's gift of salvation, and use the spaces below to mark the moment you begin your reign on earth as a child of the King.

I have asked God to forgive my sins, to come into my heart as my personal savior, and have received the gift of His salvation.

Date _____Time_____

Signature_____

For More
about Sheri Rose's
Ministry

If you would like to receive Sheri Rose Shepherd's newsletter, *Fit for Excellence,* or for more information about her ministry, booking information, or a schedule of upcoming events, please call (602) 407-8789, or write Sheri Rose at 15111 N. Hayden Road, Suite 160-242, Scottsdale, AZ 85260.

Sheri Rose and her husband, Steve, also publish *Christian Health* magazine, the nation's first publication addressing health, nutrition, exercise, healing, and medicine from a godly perspective.

...More Books On Getting Ready
For Life

Still Lickin' the Spoon
& Other Confessions of a Grown-Up Kid
Becky Freeman

In her fourth book for Broadman & Holman, best-selling humorist Becky Freeman shows how childlike truths can mirror deeper human emotions. This collection of stories offers a humorous, uplifting, and childlike view of life that appeals to all ages.   0-8054-6279-1

Tiptionary
Mary Hunt

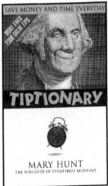

Once again, Mary Hunt proves that saving money can be fun. *Tiptionary* is packed with innovative and inexpensive solutions to all sorts of everyday challenges, from dealing with bored children to ring around the collar. These clever tips for virtually painless economizing will leave readers saying, "What a great idea!"   0-8054-0147-4

The Financially Confident Woman
Mary Hunt

Financial trouble is not a money problem; it's an attitude problem. "This is not a book about budgets," writes author Mary Hunt. "It is about how to identify irresponsible financial behaviors and change them forever." Once women realize they can be successful stewards of their resources, regardless of their income, the journey toward financial security can begin.   0-8054-6285-6

AVAILABLE AT FINE CHRISTIAN BOOKSTORES EVERYWHERE

...More Books On Getting Ready
For Life

Saving Graces
The Inspirational Writings of Laura Ingalls Wilder
Edited by Stephen Hines

This collection of highlights from the writings of Laura Ingalls Wilder is aglow with Wilder's ability to sense a divine presence in everyday things. The girl who grew up on the plains never forgot how to cherish the little blessings of life. As a woman, she continued to marvel at the gifts of God and the wonder of the world around her. This entertaining and inspiring book is a thoughtful gift idea for all ages. 0-8054-0148-2

Building Strong Families
Dr. William Mitchell & Michael Mitchell

The most important strategy parents can employ for building strong families is to build a legacy of love. Based on Proverbs 22:6 ("Train up a child in the way he should go, and when he is old, he will not depart from it"), this book explores the characteristics of a strong family, the importance of parental leadership, parenting philosophies and setting family goals. It also teaches how a legacy of love can equip families to weather unexpected tragedies. 0-8054-6370-4

The Woman Behind The Mirror
Finding Inward Satisfaction with Your Outward Appearance
Judith Couchman

Throughout their lives, women are pressured to meet society's unrealistic standards of physical perfection. The result is an obsession with their appearance that prevents many women from becoming personally and spiritually fulfilled. This book encourages them to celebrate their physical appearance rather than worry about reaching an artificial, impossible ideal. 0-8054-6077-2

A Tender Road Home
The Story of How God Healed a Marriage Crippled by Anger and Abuse
Paul & Susie Luchsinger

He was a rodeo champion. She was a promising country singer. But behind the big smiles and bright lights, their marriage was dying. Paul and Susie lived in a world of violence, selfishness and manipulation. Peace and happiness remained beyond their grasp until they turned humbly to God for help. At that moment the healing began, and two newly dedicated Christians took their first steps along *A Tender Road Home*. 0-8054-6082-9

AVAILABLE AT FINE CHRISTIAN BOOKSTORES EVERYWHERE